The Highway Code for Parenting

Published 2007 by CWR, Waverley Abbey House, Waverley
Lane, Farnham, Surrey GU9 8EP, UK.

See back of book for list of National Distributors.

Unless otherwise indicated, all Scripture references are from
the Holy Bible: New International Version (NIV), copyright ©
1973, 1978, 1984 by the International Bible Society.

Concept development, editing, design and production by CWR

Printed in Croatia by Zrinski

ISBN-13: 978-1-85345-419-6
ISBN-10: 1-85345-419-2

The
Highway Code
for Parenting

Michael & Hilary Perrott

Introduction

This is for you if you are –

- becoming a parent
- feeling overwhelmed
- struggling with issues
- enjoying the family

To *become* a parent you need no licence, take no exam, pass no test. But *being* a parent is the most challenging and rewarding job in the world. If the child who has arrived in your home is your first, you are on the steepest learning curve you will ever encounter. Life will *never* be the same again.

THIS TINY SCRAP OF HUMANITY IS UNIQUE. There is no other fingerprint just like his. Among a billion people her eyeprint is not duplicated. She's special – and she's yours. Yours to care for, yours to guide and above all yours to love. As you gaze in awe at the baby in your arms you prize being a parent more highly than being president or queen.

But that is just the beginning. Those with years of parenting behind them will have played the role of resident nurse, hotel manager, taxi driver, interpreter of grunts, controller of inexhaustible funds, judge, jury, jailor, referee, psychologist, cook, counsellor, comforter and friend. The roles are interchangeable at the drop of a hat and all jobs are unpaid. Yet some of you do it again and again.

WHAT MAKES THEM WHAT THEY BECOME? Nature? Straight hair or wavy; blue eyes or brown; strong willed or compliant? Guess where they got these things? If you didn't believe in heredity you do now! Nurture? About nature you can do nothing; you've done it already! About nurture you will do everything you can to give your child an environment in which he or she can thrive.

You will have failures and disappointments, cloudy days and stormy, days when you think your heart cannot contain the pride and tenderness you feel for son or daughter. Sometimes there will be pain behind the mask you wear, at others a joy you want to share with the world. The pendulum swings from hard slog for which the only longed-for remedy is sleep, to sheer delight in bonding with your child.

The *person you are* influences more than anything else the *parent you become*. It is an awesome thought that your words and actions, good or bad, your children will remember long after they have flown the nest and built their own. Try to live so that when they are grown and perhaps *look down on you*, they may also be able to *look up to you* with respect forged over the years.

TOPS AND PITS. Your greatest difficulty will be managing time. You will learn to plan when you can and juggle when you can't. Your greatest challenge will be change. The small child who thinks you know everything becomes a teenager who is sure you know nothing. You're tops and pits. There are no quick fixes or easy answers. Fathers will get used to 'no!' at two years of age, 'why?' at three, and 'Dad, can I have?' most of the rest of the time. Did you think a mother was a human with two hands and two feet? Wrong! She is an octopus crossed with an air traffic controller.

THE OPPORTUNITY OF A LIFETIME. Being a mother or father is a responsibility like no other and with each child you have only one chance to get it right. It is literally true that 'the opportunity of a lifetime must be taken within the lifetime of the opportunity'. They didn't ask to be born and you didn't consult them! Make sure they know you're glad they're here.

The opportunity of a lifetime must be taken within the lifetime of the opportunity

MEMO

A PARENT GUIDE WITH A DIFFERENCE. This is a parent guide with a difference. It's written in note form which can be dipped into or read through in one sitting. It doesn't deal with details of toilet training or pocket money, but with the 'biggies' of good parenting. It's about love and self-esteem, discipline and development of character, equipping your children for life, dealing with hard issues and looking after yourself. Although the authors of the book have a Christian view of life, the principles outlined are applicable to people of other faiths or none. If you want academic theories go elsewhere; this is a common sense approach to common problems. You'll enter the book with the yawn of a baby and come out the other end as a grandparent! It's a guide to being a guide to your children.

A GUARANTEED FORMULA? Is there a guaranteed formula for successful parenting? No! Because no two children are the same. The boiling water which softens the turnip hardens the egg. Boys and girls have free will – and use it! Perfect parents and perfect children do not exist, and the only people who are 100 per cent sure how to bring up children are those who have not had any!

Are there no guidelines then or is it Learn As You Go? It's partly that, for you learn on the job. But yes, there are guidelines. Read on, and may *The Highway Code for Parenting* help you with problems you'll encounter and skills which can be learned. May you find joy in life's greatest privilege and courage in life's toughest task.

Contents

Absorbing your love

A

$\frac{1}{2}$m

children are sponges; love is spelt TIME; window of opportunity; art of good listening; magic of touch; what love really is; sibling rivalry; child care

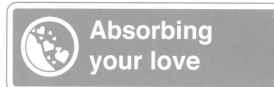

Absorbing your love

CHILDREN ARE SPONGES WHO ABSORB YOUR LOVE. They soak up the atmosphere in which they live. What they think, how they feel, how they see themselves and view their world, is affected largely by their parents. Only to a limited extent do you even teach them to speak. They absorb your words (sometimes you'll wish they hadn't!) and even your accent. They soak up your attitudes, values, standards and habits. Happy the child who absorbs your love. How is that love shown?

Love shown by time

EVERYONE IS EQUAL. Everyone is equal in the amount of time they have. Whether they live in Britain or China, America or Africa, all have exactly 1,440 minutes in their day. Not a minute more, not a minute less. It's what you *do* with your time that makes the difference. You can be so concerned to give your children the things you didn't have when you were a child, that you fail to give them the one thing you do have – your time. And you will know that children spell love TIME.

A little girl, thrilled to have her father home again after his long absence, hung on to him while he talked with a friend. He put his hand in his pocket, pulled out some coins and said, 'Go and buy yourself something.' She protested, 'Daddy, I don't want your old money, I want you.' An 18-year-old boy, the son of a wealthy man, said in a matter-of-fact tone, 'My father gave me money, but not time', and it's well known that a child wants your *presence* more than your *presents*.

Here are two scenarios. The first is a dad playing with his little son when the child's mother comes into the room and says, 'Joe Brown is on the phone for you.' Dad gets up and goes to the phone. Twenty minutes later he's back to find his son has lost interest and disappeared. The second scenario starts in the same way – father, son and telephone. But this time the dad says, 'Tell him I have someone with me and I'll phone back later.' Which boy gets the message, 'I'm important to my Dad'?

A child wants your presence more than your presents

MEMO

QUALITY WITHOUT QUANTITY? Do we use the old excuse, 'I'm busy, but I make sure I give quality time to my kids'? Quality without quantity? Impossible! What restaurant would survive if it served the most delicious meal (all of one square inch) to its customers? It is possible to have a suppose-I-must-put-up-with-you quantity of time with the kids, which clearly has no quality about it, but I-like-being-involved-with-you quality time is not enough unless it comes in substantial quantities. There needs to be more than a few words exchanged during ads on TV.

A man writing to his mother for her birthday said, 'When I think back to my childhood, you were always there, not spoiling us but always giving us your time. I remember the swimming, the walks, the games, and not much of when you were exhausted.' Many years later that's what he remembered, 'you were always there … giving us your time'. You can have time without love, but not love without time.

MEMO

You can have time without love, but not love without time

BARRIERS TO FAMILY TIME

○ **The job.** A mother confessed, 'If I'm honest, I have to admit the problem wasn't my work: it was me. I loved my work and let it consume me, and it nearly consumed my children.' The greatly admired pastor of a large congregation reflected sadly at the end of his ministry, 'I built a church and lost a family.'

Children don't care what their father's job is, whether he's a judge or a joiner, or if their mother's a hairdresser, nurse or company director, but they do mind if they don't have their parent's time. It's possible to be cash-rich and time-poor. A man changed jobs and settled for a lower salary so he wouldn't have to spend so much time travelling to and from work. 'It boiled down to this,' he explained, 'when I saw it was a straight choice between hours in the car or time with the kids, it was easy.'

○ **The home.** A perfect house is a perfect nuisance if it means that children get brushed away with the dust. You can have everything in place yet no place for a child to be a child. One couple who realised their priorities had been wrong said, 'We were rattling round in a big house with a mortgage we couldn't afford. Then we wised up, sold the house and bought a smaller one. Now we have both the time and money to enjoy the family, and the difference in the children is amazing. We have a lot of fun. Best thing we ever did!' The wife added, 'There's less to clean!'

○ **Outside commitments.** Hobbies, sport and other interests, the very things which can enrich the lives of parents, can deprive the children of time. One boy referred to his dad as 'Mr Meeting'. It's a question of balance. A father opted for playing at a lower level in his sports club because that meant less training and more time at home.

Busyness is the enemy of relationship. If you are too busy to spend time with your children, you are too busy. To be busy *sometimes* is unavoidable, to be *always too busy* is a choice.

Busyness is the enemy of relationship

MEMO

WINDOW OF OPPORTUNITY

Vincent Foster, an outstanding lawyer and a counsel to the President of the United States, when giving the commencement speech to the graduating class at the University of Arkansas School of Law, reminded the students that 'no one was ever heard to say on their death-bed, "I wish I had spent more time at the office."' He went on, 'Balance wisely your professional life and your family life. If you are fortunate to have children, your parents will warn you that they will grow up and be gone before you know it. I can testify that is true. God only allows us so many opportunities with our children to read a story, go fishing, play catch and say our prayers together. Try not to miss one of them. The office can wait. It will still be there after your children have gone.' Within weeks Vince Foster was dead. He was forty-eight.

Vince Foster said, 'read a story'. Do that. There is something special about a parent or grandparent reading to the children. As they curl up on your knee or stretch out in their bed, your voice and their imagination combine to bring them into another world. It is something you and they will never forget. You are giving them your time and with it they absorb your love. Read to them, read with them, let them read to you. You don't have to be rich to give them a love of reading, and reading is an open door to an open mind, and an open mind is an open door to a balanced life.

Talk to them. Research shows there is a period between eight and eighteen months which can be crucial in a child's life. The amount of interaction and live language directed to children at this time can influence their mental and social development in years to come. One busy mother with three daughters goes out for breakfast with one of the girls each week, and an equally busy father of four alternated doing something, of their choosing, with each of his children.

The window of opportunity is not large. When they are very young they both *need* you and *want* you. Moving up their teens they still *need* you but in their natural surge towards independence may not always *want* you. A fifteen-year-old boy was embarrassed that anyone should know that he even had a mother! With independence they may no longer *need* you, but if you have established a good relationship with them in earlier years, they will hopefully still *want* you. It is sad to hear older parents complain, 'Our children never have time for us.' Often it's not hard to guess why.

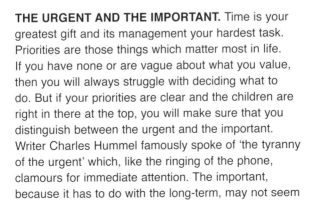

MEMO

Give time while you have it

THE URGENT AND THE IMPORTANT. Time is your greatest gift and its management your hardest task. Priorities are those things which matter most in life. If you have none or are vague about what you value, then you will always struggle with deciding what to do. But if your priorities are clear and the children are right in there at the top, you will make sure that you distinguish between the urgent and the important. Writer Charles Hummel famously spoke of 'the tyranny of the urgent' which, like the ringing of the phone, clamours for immediate attention. The important, because it has to do with the long-term, may not seem demanding; whereas the 'urgent' may not in fact be important. You only have a certain quantity of time and no day or hour can ever be repeated. Learn to say 'no' to the trivial and 'now' to the children. Give time while you have it.

If it's important to them, it's important!

MEMO

Love shown by listening

SEEN BUT NOT HEARD. No one would accept today that 'children should be seen and not heard', but one teenager said, 'I feel as if my parents can see me through a window but can't hear me, and I long to be heard.' A couple with two daughters and two sons are very clear that there is a difference between the needs and nurturing of boys and girls. They sum it up this way, 'Girls need you to listen and talk; boys need you to listen and do.' Either way you show your love by listening.

o **Be on their level.** Eye to eye is more likely to be felt as heart to heart than if you are looking over their head. Especially when they are small it is good to sit, squat or kneel so they are not distanced by your size or height.

o **Be interested in their interests.** You may not care much for their music, but don't mock it. Listen to it – sometimes! When you do, in a way you are listening to them. You may not aspire to becoming an authority on stick insects, but if it interests them, then know enough to ask questions. You may not like their likes, but listen to them, for if it's important to them, it's important!

o **Focus on their feelings.** Her words were, 'She didn't ask me to her party', her feeling was rejection. He said, 'I've been picked to play for the school.' What did he feel?

o **Relay back meaning and emotions.** 'You're saying that? … You feel that ..?' Asking questions like these helps *you* to understand them, and helps *them* to know you really want to understand, and that you care.

o **Invite them to share their feelings.** If you share your own first it may be easier for them to respond. You might say, 'I really had a bad day today. Everything seemed to go wrong. Do you feel fed up sometimes.' 'You do?' 'What sort of things make you fed up?' Children who feel listened to are more likely to open up.

o **Be non-judgmental.** They ought to be able to say anything to you so long as they do so respectfully. You may think their views are way out, but if you dismiss them as rubbish they (teenagers especially) are more likely to defend them. Remember the views they express may not be their views at all, and they may just be checking on yours!

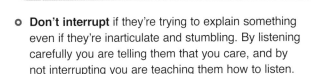

MEMO

'A smile is a curve that puts a lot of things straight!'

o **Don't interrupt** if they're trying to explain something even if they're inarticulate and stumbling. By listening carefully you are telling them that you care, and by not interrupting you are teaching them how to listen.

o **Match their mood.** Laugh with them, cry with them. When *your* face and voice reflect how *they* feel, they know they're loved. Match their mood, and sometimes just smile for no reason at all. Remember 'a smile is a curve that puts a lot of things straight!'

Love shown by touch

THE MAGIC OF TOUCH. To touch and be touched is magic for a baby. Look at her as she explores her parent's face. The nose is pushed, the hair pulled, the lips parted, the cheek prodded. She goes into gales of laughter as she feels a gentle blow of breath on her skin. Hear the sigh of contentment as she nestles against the face she has come to know and trust. She smiles at the recognised touch of the hand that strokes her, and yawns happily in the arms that hold her. As she absorbed nourishment from her mother in the womb so now she absorbs love through your touch.

TOUCH OUTGROWN? When a child outgrows cot and pram he has not outgrown the need of touch. When he falls, caring arms 'make it better'. He feels secure walking hand in hand, encouraged by your arm on his shoulder or assured in the cradled comfort of your lap. Some are more tactile than others but nearly all children, girls as well as boys, enjoy rough-housing with their dads. Around puberty some children pull away, but if a natural wholesome touch can be maintained, it can help in the teenage years and beyond. The 'safe' touch of home with which they are familiar can protect them against the wrong kind of touch with the wrong person.

STRUGGLE WITH TOUCH. Talking about touch a woman explained, 'As I look back I cannot remember being kissed or cuddled or even touched by my mother.' A lack of touch in childhood may lead to the child-become-adult finding it hard to express affection physically to *her* children, and that can go unrecognised from generation to generation.

Love shown by telling

The familiar voice of the parent is the sound of safety for a child. The boy coming home shouts 'Mum', and is reassured by her answering call. But you can't assume they know you love them if you don't tell them. They need to know you love them not *if* or *when* or *because* they do something. Not *if* they win, or *when* they are good or *because* they succeed. Win or lose, good or bad, success or failure, you love them. Your love is unconditional. There are no strings attached.

For some, the words 'I love you' don't come easily. A man, with some embarrassment, tells how his young wife would look up at him and ask entreatingly, 'Do you love me?' and he would look down at her with, 'Of course I do, I married you, didn't I?' He went on to explain that he grew up in a home where love was not openly expressed so when he married it took him several years before 'I love you' came easily.

Just as flowers can't grow without water and cars can't go without fuel so children can't live without love. They may survive, but they'll not thrive. The fact that *you* know that you love them doesn't mean *they* automatically feel it. A variation of what the Scots say is, 'Love is more felt when it's telt!'

Love is ...

'All you need is love,' sang the Beatles, but what is love? It is practically impossible to define, but these are some of its characteristics.

LOVE IS SAFE. A child can say anything – anything. 'Daddy, is there a lion in there?' Dad opens the door of the cupboard under the stairs and checks that there is no lion. 'Mum, I didn't like the way the man touched me.' 'Tell me about it,' she answers, 'where did he touch you?' Home is a place of refuge from the outside world. Laughed at in school the child comes through the door and bursts into tears. It's OK to cry. She's been dumped by her best friend, he's not sure he'll be picked for the team, a lot depends on the exams, he feels desperately unsure. There's no hurt too deep or fear too great to share. Love is safe.

LOVE SETS LIMITS. A child can't do anything he wants or have everything he'd like. Down that road he would become a menace to society and to himself. There are two words at the heart of parental love, one is 'yes' and the other 'no'. 'Yes, I will always love you', and 'no, there are limits to what you can do'. It is the 'yes' that leads to 'no'. '*Because* I love you I will not let you hurt yourself or others.' Love sets limits.

> *Because* I love you I will not let you hurt yourself or others

MEMO

LOVE IS FAIR. In the best sense a parent is predictable because consistent. The children know where you stand. You have no favourites. In inter-sibling warfare the court of appeal (that's you) will hand down a careful and clear decision. Love is fair.

LOVE IS DOING. Love is more than feeling, it's doing. It's singing to your baby, clapping hands, talking to him (football if you like, cooking if you prefer; he won't understand a word but he's drinking in your love like mother's milk). Love is what you *do* whether you feel like it or not. Up nine times in one night with a sick child? Did you *enjoy* it? Of course not. But you did it anyway and though you crawl into the morning like a zombie you are *glad* you were there for your child. Love is doing.

LOVE IS THOUGHTFUL. If bedtime (say) is coming up give them warning. When they're small they don't have the same concept of time as you do, and from their viewpoint you are unreasonably interrupting their play. Countdowns get them used to the idea and make bedtime less of a battle. Love is thoughtful.

LOVE PROTECTS. Love warns … it looks round corners … it's alert for danger. If a child cannot defend herself, love leaps to do so. Love protects.

LOVE IS WISE. A parent's instinct is to protect a child from hurt and harm, but don't handicap your child by making life too sheltered. In life's buffetings support is better than prevention. When you teach a child to ride a bike you walk (or run) behind holding the back of the saddle. You take your hand off for a few seconds and then when he wobbles you grasp it again. But in the end you let go. He will fall sometimes, but then falling is part of learning. The wisdom of love is balancing 'hands on' with 'hands off'. Love is wise.

LOVE IS HONEST. Answer their questions truthfully, remembering that truthfully does not mean hurtfully. Your child proudly shows you a drawing of what looks like an alien from outer space, which turns out to be you! Do you like it? Of course you do. But never lie to your children; if you do they may copy you. Besides if they find you out when you don't tell the truth they will doubt you when you do tell it. Love is honest.

> **MEMO**
> **Don't handicap your child by making life too sheltered**

LOVE IS GIVING. Counsellors agree that one of the hardest people to help is an adult spoiled rotten as a child. Parents who spoil their children *feel* they are being kind, but in *fact* sow a 'mine' field – my way, rights, feelings, wishes, views. She was a wise woman who said, 'Give them everything they need, not everything they want!' Love is giving.

LOVE IS FUN. Go crazy … let your hair down … unbend … have a laugh … be adventurous … do something different … make a face … join in their play. If you have more than one child do something of *their* choosing with each of them. Love is fun.

LOVE IS OPEN. Sometimes behaviour needs to be challenged, but because eye-to-eye contact might seem threatening to her teens, one mother would pick moments when driving alone with one of them in the car. Doing it like this she found she could deal with big issues in a non-confrontational way. Love is open.

> ## Some of the deepest questions come at the oddest times
>
> MEMO

LOVE IS 'THERE'. Some of the deepest questions come at the oddest times. Kicking a ball in the park – 'Dad, when did God begin?' Washing her teeth before going to bed – 'Mum, where did I come from?' They asked because they felt like asking – and you were there. And they know you'll never say, 'What a stupid question.' Love is 'there'.

LOVE IS UNCONDITIONAL. It is not 'I will love you if you are a good boy'. It is not dependent on whether they pass their exams, win a race, keep their room tidy, always say 'thank you', go to church, come in on time at night. Love is not linked to expectation or governed by achievement. It is not dependent on size, looks, IQ or success. Love is unconditional.

Note: Many women experience 'baby blues' with mood swings for the first few days after having a baby, but if the feelings don't disappear you should check with your doctor. Postnatal depression is not your fault; many women experience it. If you don't have strong feelings of love for your baby at first, don't be too concerned; as you give yourself to your baby, they'll come!

Love and siblings

They heard silence. Now when you have a toddler and a crawler in a room for any length of time, and you hear silence, there is something wrong. Mum and Dad rushed from the kitchen into the sitting room to find one child where there should have been two.

> Parents, desperately, to toddler …
> 'Kevin, where's John?' No answer.
> 'Where … is … John?' Silence.
> 'Quickly Kevin, where's John?'
> 'I dropped him.'
> 'You dropped him! Where did you drop him?'
> 'Out of the window.'

The parents exploded from house to garden and found crawler in the flowerbed meditatively sucking a stone and none the worse for his involuntary and rapid descent.

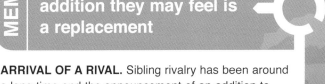

MEMO

What you regard as an addition they may feel is a replacement

ARRIVAL OF A RIVAL. Sibling rivalry has been around a long time and the announcement of an addition to the family may not be met with enthusiasm. A mother, expecting a baby around Christmas, asked her little son, 'Which would you like, a little brother or a little sister?' The boy answered, 'Actully, I'd rather have a bikykle.' When the new baby comes a lot of attention is diverted to the new arrival. It's hardly surprising as mum and dad have exactly the same amount of time as they did before – not a minute more – and much less energy. Thumb sucking, bed-wetting, baby talk and temper tantrums can be a demand for attention, and a protest at (it seems) being ousted. What you regard as an addition they may feel is a replacement.

ADOPTION. If in your family you have a biological child and an adopted one let them know they are equal in your love. Make sure that the adopted child knows early on about his or her adoption. A man in his forties, finding it necessary to apply for a full birth certificate, stared unbelievingly at it. Adopted? Is this person *me*? *Why* didn't they tell me? Who am I?' Whatever the good intentions of the adoptive parents may be, later discovery is devastating.

CONFLICT IS INEVITABLE. Conflict between sisters and brothers is inevitable and justified by, 'he hit me', 'it's not fair', 'she did it first', 'you gave him three minutes more than me', 'that's mine', 'I hate him', 'she put her foot inside my room …' But you can't intervene all the time; nor should you try. If it's only a squabble it's best they sort it out themselves. But there's a difference between bickering and all-out aggression, and if World War III breaks out you may have to protect or defend so no harm is done physically or emotionally. Conflict between siblings which is a pain for the parent is necessary for the children. The disadvantage an only child has is that there is no one to practise on!

SIBLING RIVALRY is a natural phenomenon but made worse by:

○ **Flawed justice.** An older child takes advantage of age and size and bullies the younger, or is rendered powerless by a parent who won't allow self-defence against harassment 'because he's smaller'. By the time No.3 comes along Nos.1 and 2 think, 'we were never allowed that at her age; she can get away with murder'. Privately the 'good' son or daughter who gives no trouble may feel aggrieved that the 'troublemaker' in the family gets all the attention.

Sometimes, of course, justice can be flawed because the judge is exhausted!

Favouritism is wrong. It can be the root of resentment and the death of love. Take care not only to have no favourite but be *seen* to have no favourite.

MEMO

Take care not only to have no favourite but to be *seen* to have no favourite

- **Unfair comparison.** Be careful not to compare a child with sisters or brothers (or other children), especially in the areas of intelligence, looks or skill.
  - A father refers to Joe's young brother – 'he's the bright one in our family,' and Joe overhearing interprets, 'he's got the brains and I'm just dumb.'
  - A mother speaks of Jill's sister as – 'the pretty one,' and Jill thinks, 'if she's the pretty one, what does that make me?'
  - A father enthuses about Tom's brother –- 'now he's the one with the ball skills,' and Tom concludes, 'Dad doesn't think I'm any good.'

What's the outcome? Resentment and jealousy. None of those parents meant to hurt their children, but all of them did.

BE EVEN-HANDED. It will test your ingenuity, but keep trying.

- **Give praise generously** to your child in private but put limits on the amount of praise you give in front of brothers and sisters.

- **Give lots of reassurance.** 'I love you, Sally, so much. You know, when you were as small as Tom, I did exactly the same for you as I'm doing for him now. But you can do things now he can't. And I'm really proud of you.'

o **Get them involved.** 'Would you help me for a moment with Tom? Then we'll do something together.'

Love and childcare

The majority of mothers say they would not work outside the home when their child is young if they didn't have to. But for many it is not an option. Childcare may take many forms – other mothers, grandparents, aunts, nannies and day-care centres.

DAY-CARE CENTRES

o **Check it out.** Is it registered? What are the credentials of those who run it and the qualifications of the staff? What is the staff-to-child ratio? For 0–2 years it should be about 1:3, from 2–3 years 1:4, from 3–5 years 1:8.

o **Ask around.** Talk with parents who have had children there. What are they saying?

o **Look around.**
  - When you visit the place does it look safe, clean and well equipped?
  - Do the children look occupied and happy?
  - Do the staff seem calm, confident and loving with the children? You are concerned not only with competence but also character.

Mothers may feel guilty about leaving their child and going out to work, but then they may feel guilty staying at home and not going out to work. Be guided by your love and what is best for them and you as well as your wider life circumstances.

Love as your greatest gift

The greatest gift you can give your children is your love. Let it flow from you so they absorb it into the very fabric of their being. Let it be the air they breathe and the milk they drink, so they *feel* it long before they *understand* it. It is on the foundation of your love they build their life.

Building their self-esteem

B ¹2m

everyone needs three legs; sticks and
stones; building blocks of self-esteem;
security, appearance, responsibility;
constructive criticism; the practice of praise

Building their self-esteem

EVERYONE NEEDS THREE LEGS! You can safely rest your full weight on a stool which has three strong legs of equal length. It is well known that the three basic emotional needs of a person are:

- **The need to feel loved** and with it the sense of belonging
- **The need to feel accepted** and with it the sense of worth
- **The need to feel adequate** and with it the sense of achievement

The first was dealt with in the previous chapter and the second and third are covered in this chapter. Where all three needs are met there will be a strong and stable person. Everyone needs three legs.

Self-esteem is the way you see yourself and what you believe about yourself. It is massively important and affects both character and behaviour. The single biggest factor in building a healthy self-esteem is when a child sees herself positively through the eyes of her parents. That need is profound and there are grown men and women who are still looking for the approval of long-dead parents.

Hurt and harm

NICKNAMES can be fun – and hurtful. A man tells that he was called 'Big Ears' when a boy, and a woman how she was known sometimes as 'Aeroplane Legs'. There was nothing out of the ordinary about his ears or her legs, but feelings of awkwardness and embarrassment dogged them into adult years. No wonder psychologist

Dr James Dobson, Founder and President of Focus on the Family, writes, 'The self-concept of a child is extremely fragile, and must be handled with great care.'

WRONG LABELS. It's one thing to say, 'That's a stupid thing to do', for that describes behaviour, but if you say '*You're* stupid', you are putting a label on the child. Say it often enough and they'll believe you, and will be launched into life with feelings which say, 'That's me, I'm bound to mess it up'. Call them clumsy and their self-confidence may be so dented that they actually become clumsy.

STICKS AND STONES. 'Sticks and stones may break my bones but words can never hurt me' is the most foolish of all sayings. Cuts and bruises may heal in days but wounds caused by words can lie open for a lifetime. A man in his forties, with tears in his eyes, told how his father would dismiss him with, 'You're pathetic.' He added, 'I've lived in the shadow of those words ever since.' A teenage girl overheard her mother saying to a friend, 'Of course she isn't nearly as pretty as her sister.' As an adult she *never* looked in a mirror without hearing those words, and *never* believed those who assured her otherwise.

Your sarcastic throwaway, 'were you born in a barn?' (*you* ought to know the answer to that!), comparisons like, 'your sister always did' and your stinging 'you'll never manage it' rocks their self-esteem. 'I wish you had never been born' says, 'I don't want you and you're a burden to me.' Spoken carelessly or in the heat of the moment, words can haunt a person for the rest of his or her life.

EXPECTATIONS. There are parents who drive their children to excel in everything; it's not enough to be good, their sons and daughters must be the best. Why? Is it really for their child's sake, or is it for their own as they take credit for their child's success? Because they hover over every part of their children's lives they have been called 'helicopter parents' who have offspring who *know* more than they *grow*. As people they remain stunted by the downward force of parental pressure.

Nothing is worse for a child than seeking in vain for the approval of unpleasable parents. Unrealistic expectations can lead *them* to feeling stupid (that they didn't perform properly) and *you* feeling angry (because they didn't try). Don't expect more from them than they are capable of at their age and stage. Children develop at different rates. Some are running round at nine months and others haven't discovered legs till eighteen months. A boy at fifteen years of age was bottom of the class, at eighteen he was top. Flowers don't all open on the same day.

> **MEMO**
>
> ## Flowers don't all open on the same day

The building blocks of self-esteem

LOVE. A man looking back on his childhood said, 'My father died when I was nine. Because of his work, and later because moving was so much in my mother's blood, I had been to six schools by the time I was twelve, and by eighteen years of age had lived in twenty different houses. Yet I grew up secure and confident for there was one constant, one absolute in my life, which was my mother's love. Love was her greatest gift to me.'

SECURITY. Why did that man feel secure while he was growing up? Because he was loved and because he belonged – '*my* mother, *my* brother, *my* sister, *my* family' and later '*my* friends'. If love and belonging make for security, anxiety and fear make for its opposite. For children who are constantly worried about what is happening in their world, it may not be easy to develop a positive outlook. Abuse or bullying is devastating for children of any age, but they will survive if they know that you will constantly support and vigorously defend them.

KNOWLEDGE. Self-esteem is a fragile thing and if their ignorance is met with a contemptuous 'you didn't know *that*!' from their peers, children will feel that you failed them – and particularly if you hadn't given them the basics of sex. Whatever family terms you have for the sexual organs make sure they know the real ones. Confidence grows with knowledge.

COMMUNICATION. It makes for confidence if they can 'hold their own' in conversation. One woman said, 'I'm sure my reluctance to join in chat comes from all the times I was shouted down as a child. I'm afraid of saying the wrong thing!' Ask children what they think and listen to what they say. The easy sociability of the parent influences the ability of the child to mix with people of different ages and from all walks of life. Let busy parents who regard their home as a sanctuary to get away from people, take care not to isolate their children from the world into which they are growing.

The possibility of losing makes winning exciting

MEMO

ACHIEVEMENT. There are slow starters and slow learners. Winston Churchill twice failed to get into the Royal Military Academy at Sandhurst and Albert Einstein failed his first attempt at the entrance examination to the Polytechnic in Zurich. When he was young the parents of Bill Gates were concerned that he was underachieving.

Try to find something your son or daughter is good at and encourage that. A teenage boy, upset that he had no ball skills and couldn't run fast, discovered that he could run long. As he became an outstanding long-distance runner his attitude to himself changed dramatically. Whatever you do don't try to protect them from competition; it's part of life. The possibility of losing makes winning exciting.

If they haven't done a chore or job perfectly, so long as you know they have done their best, don't you do it over again. As they get bigger how long does it take to say, 'You can do this now as well as (or better than) I can'? Seconds? The impact may last for years. If possible get them to teach *you* something.

APPEARANCE. Is this your nineteen-year-old daughter coming down the stairs? Sorry, she's fourteen actually, but has just aged five years in the last hour – and so have you! Who's at the door, a stranger or a recently revised version of your son? Most of the time you button your lips, sit on your hands and accept the experiments. If you have to draw a line remember that though they groan they may be glad (sometimes!) to use their parents as an excuse for not doing something they don't want to do.

How they appear to their peers matters a lot and some of them will need plenty of encouragement during the acne years. About 80 per cent of teenagers are uncomfortable with some aspect of their appearance, too tall, too small, too fat, too thin, braces on teeth, spots on chin; so be positive and draw attention to their bonus points. Dads, if you think your daughter is lovely, tell her. She needs to hear it from you.

POSITIVE THINKING. There is evidence that at a ratio of 9 to 1 successful people focus on *solutions* rather than *problems*, while those who do not succeed dwell at the same ratio on *problems* rather than *solutions*. Henry Ford, a man of little education but extraordinary ability, grinned, 'Whether you think that you can, or that you can't, you are usually right!' One of the greatest obstacles to getting things done is the negative mindset of 'I can't do it'. Encourage your kids to think positively, 'I'll have a go', and if they fail, 'I'll have another go'.

CLEAR GOALS. You will help your children think through their priorities without which they will wobble through life. And they need clear goals. Set too high they will become discouraged, set too low they will not be challenged. If they have too many goals there will be tough choices to make, for there is not time in one life to do everything. They must be selective to be effective, and growth is gradual.

INTERESTS. Help them cultivate a wide range of interests. Within reason the more things they are involved in the less they'll be bored, and the less they are bored the less likely they are to 'go with the crowd'. As their knowledge and experience increases so confidence grows.

Giving responsibility says, 'I can count on you.'

MEMO

RESPONSIBILITY. Nothing matures children so effectively as having responsibility, so long as it is appropriate to age. A mother said, 'I did everything for them because it was easier.' Was it strange that the children grew up self-focused and unreliable? Responsibility builds their self-esteem; give it to them. The fact that you know that they *can* do it and trust them that they *will* do it says, 'I can count on you.'

INDEPENDENCE. At first you make the choices for them, then you give them limited choices such as 'Do you want to play with this toy or that one?' As you gradually extend the range of choices they can make, you'll find their decisions aren't always yours. Eventually you are simply in an advisory role with regard to what clothes they'll wear or what subjects they'll study. There may be no formal Declaration of Independence, but the time comes when they are confident enough to make their own decisions including which career to follow or person to marry.

PARENTAL SELF-ESTEEM. How a parent (particularly the mother) feels about herself has been shown to impact her child profoundly. Be positive, look after yourself, talk yourself up not down. The happier and more confident you are as a parent, the happier and more confident your child is likely to be.

Constructive criticism

Negative criticism is destructive and leaves a child feeling guilty, apprehensive and rebellious. But a parent must not hold back on necessary and constructive criticism. So how do you go about it? The same way as you would hope to receive it.

PRIVATELY. Place: when no one else is present, especially not in front of their friends. Time: not first thing in the morning, not last thing at night, not when either of you is tired.

POSITIVELY. Begin with a positive comment – 'you've been a great help in the house recently, but yesterday …'

SPECIFICALLY. Not so much, 'you are so irresponsible the way you leave things lying around,' but 'when you come home from school I would really like you to put your gear away.' Limit the criticism to one item at a time.

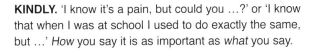

MEMO

How you say it is as important as *what* you say

KINDLY. 'I know it's a pain, but could you …?' or 'I know that when I was at school I used to do exactly the same, but …' *How* you say it is as important as *what* you say.

The practice of praise

PRAISE DIRECT. There are psychologists who say people need four (some say ten) positive comments for each negative one they receive. Whichever is the case let your affirmation heavily outweigh your criticism. If you did not receive praise face to face as a child you may find it difficult to give as an adult, even to your own children. The secret is to give it, even if you have to give it consciously and deliberately, until praise becomes reflex. Then it is no longer an 'ought to' but a 'want to'.

o **Be generous.** Praise says 'I noticed!' and parental approval is massively important to a child. If it reinforces what or when he has done well, he is more likely to do it again! Praise, because it warms the heart, builds a relationship which endures. Be generous.

To be meaningful praise must be merited

o **Be positive.** Author Stephen Covey tells of giving his little son a project to do. The boy spent almost the entire day doing what (in his judgment) his father had asked. His father came home exhausted to be met by an excited boy proud of what he had done and anxious for his dad's approval. But his father's first words were, 'Why didn't you do this? Why didn't you do that?' Writing of it afterwards the father said he would never forget 'watching the light go out' in his son's eyes. Be positive.

o **Be genuine.** A mother praised her son for the excellence of his French accent. He knew better and suspected that any French person would think he was talking Japanese. Wishing to encourage she actually undermined his confidence in other things she said. To be meaningful, praise must be merited. Be genuine.

o **Be specific.** 'You did well' or 'that was good' is fine, but it helps to say *why* – 'Clever girl for brushing your teeth and getting to bed on time.' 'That took courage', 'You really thought it through', 'That was very generous', 'You're fun to be with because …' Be specific.

o **Be careful.** Don't compare. What matters most is not whether they did better than so and so, but that they did their best. Don't qualify. Show your enthusiasm for what she has done and don't tell her how she could have done better. Be careful.

o **Be encouraging.** When things don't work out well for them don't say, 'It doesn't matter.' It probably matters a lot, at least at that moment. Try, 'You've come a long way', 'Well done, I know you tried really hard', 'You're getting the hang of it', 'You're coming on', and of course, 'I'm proud of you'. Be encouraging.

PRAISE IN THEIR PRESENCE. In conversation with a friend about computers a father said, in his son's presence, 'Max knows more about these things than I do. He keeps me straight.' His son passed it off with, 'It's just stuff I learned at school', but inside he was saying, 'Thanks, Dad', and he'll remember long after his father has forgotten. A great incentive to good behaviour and the development of character is what they hear you say about them.

PRAISE IN THEIR ABSENCE. Take care about what you say about them in their absence. Some of it may get back to them. Two girls were talking and one said, 'My Mum told me your Mum says you did a great job in the house when she was sick.' There'll be times you simply must talk over some of the child-rearing problems you encounter, and it's important you can be honest and open with other parents, but don't let it all be negative. Loyalty *by* the parent makes for loyalty *to* the parent.

Loyalty *by* the parent makes for loyalty *to* the parent

MEMO

Choosing to discipline

C 1 2m

rebels or robots; drawing boundaries;
reasons for rules; don't major on minors;
mean what you say; action and consequence;
Parents United; catch your child being good

Choosing to discipline

REBELS OR ROBOTS. If your child always did what she was told, instantly and completely, you would have a nice quiet home and a very efficient robot. But you can't love a robot or be hugged by it, and most parents would rather have a sometimes-rebellious child than an always-obedient robot.

It is inevitable that as children grow they will push the boundaries and test their parents. You did too! They are on their way from childhood to adulthood, from dependence to independence, but until that happens there must be boundaries. It's not surprising that parents ask more questions about discipline than anything else, for it's the toughest part of a tough job. Too much 'freedom' shows not how much you love but how little you care. Discipline will not make your children love you less; one day they will be grateful!

MEMO Discipline will not make your children love you less; one day they will be grateful!

Getting the balance right in the teen years is especially difficult. These are the years when conversation can slow to monosyllables, 'Yeah … no … huh …' and you feel communication is improving when you get three syllables 'I dunno' and 'I forget'.

Allowance must be made for the biochemical changes that come with puberty. The glandular upheaval affects not only the body but the brain, and what emerges from the chrysalis is more like a dragon than a butterfly. The question 'Which is harder, being a teen or the parent of a teen?' has never been resolved. One thing is certain, as a parent you must learn how to be tough and tolerant at the same time. A woman had a sign in her kitchen, 'Motherhood is not for wimps'. Add fatherhood. There's no point in telling them to 'act your age' – that's exactly what they are doing!

 'Motherhood is not for wimps' MEMO

Drawing the boundaries

REASONS FOR RULES. There are reasons for rules and they are rooted in love. Love is not the opposite of discipline but the chief reason for it. Love makes it plain, 'I love you too much to allow you to harm yourself.' 'I say "no" because I care about the way you grow up.' Significantly, the Bible says, '… the LORD disciplines those he loves' (Proverbs 3:12). Rules:

○ **Protect.** Rules are the railings which give security to a child. Inside the railings there is safety, physically and emotionally. Rules protect against injury – you must not run across the road; against obesity – you cannot eat anything you want any time you want; against abuse – you must be careful of unknown people on the Internet. The great majority of young people feel that such things as smoking, drinking and what time they come home at night should *not* be left to their own discretion.

○ **Make for freedom.** One person, untaught and untested, climbs into a car, drives 100 yards and crashes. Another slowly learns the rules of the road and controls of the car, exercises due care and attention, and in a lifetime drives half a million miles safely. Which person is free? Two set out to learn the guitar. One practises when he feels like it or if he has time. Even the dog slinks out of the room. The other practises when he doesn't feel like it, makes the time to do it, and brings pleasure to himself and maybe thousands. Which person is free? Discipline *creates* freedom.

Everyone knows that life is lived forwards but understood backwards. Most children at some stage feel their parents' discipline is robbing them of freedom, but as adults they realise that it's discipline that makes freedom possible. So you must be willing to be misunderstood by your children. Someone quipped, 'In adolescence a mother's place is in the wrong!' They don't know you are acting in their best interests and they will test your love and your patience.

MEMO

You must be willing to be misunderstood by your children

o **Create respect for authority.** When you make a bad rule or don't enforce a good one you lose your child's respect. Respect for authority is born at home and is the basis for behaviour at school and in society. Teachers know that most of the troublemakers in the classroom come from homes where there is no discipline. From no respect for parent or teacher it's only a step to no respect for law.

Those who counsel adults with behavioural problems often hear them criticise their parents for their *lack* of discipline. Children want to respect their parents and if they find they can control you, they don't respect you. You have let them down.

o **Contribute to success.** If children want to excel in sport they will never succeed unless they submit to the rules of the game, the demands of the coach and the decisions of the referee. Dreams need discipline.

It's a paradox; if you want to succeed, you submit! The game of life has its rules learned at home where the parent is rule book, coach and referee.

If you want to succeed, you submit!

MEMO

○ **Lead to self-discipline.** 'I can't understand it,' she said sobbing over her rebellious teenager, 'his father and I gave him everything he wanted.' *That* was the mistake. Ill-disciplined at five he was uncontrollable at fifteen, and became insufferable to live or work with. His expectation that he could have everything he wanted, including other people's possessions, meant that in the end he exchanged home for prison. If you want a delinquent teenager, be a permissive parent.

If your son or daughter suffers for their irresponsibility, so be it. One couple tell of their frustrations in parting their teenage son from his bed in the morning. They would call, remind, cajole, sometimes five times before he stumbled downstairs for breakfast and school. Finally they said to each other, 'We're crazy', and to him they said, 'We'll call you once and if you're late for school, that's your problem.' He was late – once – then never again. Taking responsibility makes for self-discipline.

REALISTIC RULES. Don't expect perfection. If you have rules for everything, you may be an efficient policeman but you'll end up a harassed parent with a frustrated child.

○ **Rules need to be clear.** Let the rules be clear and the reasons for them, as long as it's within their understanding. 'Because I say so' and 'Don't argue' are not enough. It's better that the child knows both *what* and *why*.

o **They need to be sensible.** One mother would not allow her children to stand on the carpet in their socks for fear of fluff being transferred to it. 'Home was like prison,' a boy said, 'it was rules, rules, rules.' Keep the rule book small.

Childproof your home. If you like graffiti, leave pens and paints around; you'll not be disappointed. You can't have 'Do not touch' on every ornament. Make them untouchable by being unreachable, if not for the sake of the ornaments then for your own sanity.

MEMO

Keep the rule book small

o **They need to be fair.** Avoid impossible demands: fully potty trained at twelve months, or three hours' homework at five years! Decisions have often to be made on the spot, but house rules should only be made after thought. If they are made up on the spur of the moment they may have to be changed next day, or else doggedly enforced because a stubborn parent doesn't want to back down. Much so-called discipline has more to do with the parent's mood than the child's behaviour, and parents' problems should not be taken out on the kids.

o **They are best when positive.** If possible a 'do' is better than a 'don't'. 'Always tell the truth' rather than 'never tell lies'.

o **Don't major on minors.** An inch of hair or skirt is not worth the hassle. If you make an issue of things which are clearly not important, they'll challenge your judgment on things that are. Say 'yes' as often as you can. The more they feel you're *for* them the more they are likely to co-operate *with* you. You'll have enough important battles to fight, so don't fight unnecessary ones. Distinguish between preference and principle; your 'yes' when there is no principle at stake strengthens your 'no' when there is. Resolving a situation is better than winning an argument, but if you want a rule of thumb let it be, 'firm but flexible'.

Your 'yes' when there is no principle at stake strengthens your 'no' when there is

MEMO

○ **Family involvement.** Every home needs some kind of organisation especially if there are several people living in it. The more the children can be involved in creating the house rules the less likely they are to break them and, by and large, involvement helps commitment. So agree the rules if you can, but impose them if you need to.

○ **Rules need revision.** Your standards and expectations with regard to truth and unselfishness should never change, either for your children or yourself. But age-related rules, such as the time at which they go to bed or come in at night, will become more flexible.

Pushing the boundaries

Whatever age they are or stage they are at they will push the boundaries, and some are definitely professional boundary pushers. One such pusher (aged four) said to her mother, 'I know from your voice when you are going to say "yes".'

MEAN WHAT YOU SAY. Scenario: small boy teasing smaller sister. Mother: 'Stop doing that at once.' She goes to the phone and returns to find he is still doing it. 'Didn't I tell you to stop it? If you do that again I'll …'

and she spells out the penalty. She gets the washing out of the washer. Hears screams and comes back blazing, 'How many times do I have to tell you to stop it? If you do that again I'll …' Twenty minutes later and after five more warnings she really loses it and there are screams and tears all round. What has that mother been doing, apart from exhausting herself? She has been teaching! She has taught her daughter, 'I can't depend on Mum to protect me.' She taught her son, 'When I do wrong I can usually get away with it.' And she has taught both children to lie for they simply didn't believe her. Let 'no' mean 'no' and 'yes' mean 'yes'. One small girl was heard whispering to her smaller sister, 'You need only do what Mummy says if she really means it.' Don't make idle threats.

Speak with a 'voice of authority'. A low, firm, controlled tone is best. Practise in front of a mirror so that your face mirrors your voice. By all means say 'please', but don't plead; you're not appealing, you're telling. You expect to be obeyed.

MEMO
Don't be afraid to be firm

TANTRUMS AND TORNADOES. A human tornado spirals down the aisle of the supermarket delightedly dislodging carefully stacked tins. Forty-five heads turn enquiringly to see what you are going to do with your son. What *do* you do? Your daughter throws herself on the living-room floor kicking and screaming because you actually said 'no'. What *do* you say?' 'Come along dear little honey sweet pet lamb, please don't do that'? Give in to that kind of pressure and your child will have learned that bad behaviour works. And she'll do it again and again. If she's like that at three years of age just wait till she's thirteen! Don't store up trouble for yourself and for her. Make sure tantrums *never* pay. Don't be afraid to be firm.

If the tantrum is in a public place you will probably remove the child as quickly as possible and deal with the misbehaviour elsewhere, but if the tantrum is at home one of the best ways of dealing with it is to ignore it. It is amazing how quickly a tantrum can subside when there is no audience.

PARENTS UNITED. When one parent disciplines and the other spoils, when one is indulgent because of the strictness of the other, the child is confused. Looking back one person said, 'We could never divide our parents. We certainly tried! But what Dad said, Mum said. What Mum said, Dad said. They didn't always think alike, but to us they spoke with one voice. It gave us a lot of security and we really respected them for their loyalty to each other. They were allies.' Don't leave all the discipline to one parent. Agree the rules, then stand by them and each other.

> *Connecting* with your children makes the task of *correcting* easier

MEMO

CONSISTENCY. The rules need to be clear and the enforcement consistent. One teenage girl, grounded for a serious misdemeanour, said to her mother afterwards, 'Mum, I never thought you would stick it out!' Appeasement doesn't work; it only increases the child's determination to control.

RELATIONSHIP. Rules based on relationship make for respect, without relationship they lead to rebellion, but *connecting* with your children makes the task of *correcting* easier both for them and you.

APOLOGY. If you have been unfair or said something you later regret, say so. Your apology shows it's OK to make mistakes, that you care about how they feel and don't want anything to come between you. Far from losing face you gain respect and so a minus becomes a plus. Remember children *want* to think well of their parents and *want* to forgive them.

MANNER OF DISCIPLINE. How *you* behave when you discipline your children will affect how *they* behave.

MEMO

Catch your child in the act of being good

- **Avoidance strategy.** A young child is easily diverted so you can save yourself many exhausting battles of will simply by pointing to something else. He has a short attention span and distraction is better than conflict – for parent and child.

- **Eye contact.** There are two ways children can see from your face that you mean business. By looking them in the eye you can make sure that you have their attention. Or you might do exactly the opposite. No eye contact. You have been repeatedly challenged and you are now saying, 'I'm not interested. Case closed.'

- **Stay calm.** Shout them into silence when they are small and you'll get submission OK, but a resentful submission. Later on your shouting will be seen as loss of control and that will mean loss of respect. It's all right to show emotion, but *action* is more effective than *anger*. If you find you are beginning to lose it, take a break until you regain your cool. Staying calm shows you are in control.

- **Tell them how you feel.** Not 'You're a selfish brat', but 'We feel that …' or 'We're concerned that …' In this way you are describing yourselves, not him, and he is more likely to respond positively if he senses your love.

o **Be positive.** Avoid nagging. Neither the nagger nor the nagged like it. How about saying, 'I'm glad that you put everything away,' rather than, 'I'm glad that just for once you put everything away without my having to ask.' It has been wisely said that you should try to catch your child in the act of being good!

DISTINGUISH BETWEEN

o **Your child and her behaviour.** Distinguish between the child and her behaviour. You can tell her that her *behaviour* is bad or foolish but make sure that she knows *she* is accepted and loved.

o **Your child and his childishness.** Distinguish between your child and his childishness. In the age of exploration he may wash his teeth with washing-up liquid, spray the hamster with perfume or experiment on the fascinating effects of gravity on cups and vases.

o **Two kinds of cries.** Most parents learn to be good interpreters and soon discover there are two kinds of cries. One is the 'I'm wet, hungry or sick' cry, to which you are happy to respond. The other is the 'I intend to get my way' cry, which is aimed at grinding you down till you give in. Don't!

o **Rewards and bribes.** There is nothing wrong with rewards. There are wages for work, awards for long service, medals for bravery. If a child is behaving badly in the supermarket and is offered a sweet to stop, that's a bribe. It is also reinforcing bad behaviour. But rewards work, that's why society gives them. A star chart or stickers can work wonders for small people.

But you can be conned. During a family holiday by the sea a father offered financial incentive to his son when he was learning to swim, so much for so many strokes. As his son swam parallel to the beach his father stood counting. He expected a couple of hundred; there were 1,200. The father was both delighted and devastated, for the reward made a considerable hole in a tight holiday budget. More than twenty years later his son confessed he had had his foot on the ground most of the time!

MANAGEMENT OF TIME. Get them into 'just doing it' whether they feel like it or not. It's a life lesson. (See the authors' book *Just Do It*, CWR.)

o **Homework.** If you don't push them enough they'll feel you don't care; if you push them too hard they'll feel you're not fair. Some are so motivated you can't keep them from their homework! But most need a break from school work and there is a (controlled) place for telephone, TV and computer games. Know what homework they are supposed to be doing, make sure they do it neatly and completely, but don't do it for them. And make sure that two hours' 'homework' is not one hour homework and one hour MSN!

o **Chores.** Whatever arrangements you come to, stick to them. It may be easier and quicker to do it yourself. Don't! You'll do them a great disservice. They need to share the responsibility of running a home.

o **Mealtimes.** It's most unfair on a parent who has carefully prepared a meal if a son or daughter saunters in late or doesn't arrive at all. Train them that if something unexpected crops up they should let you know.

o **In at night.** Be tough on this. Establish a set time (extended with age) with possible exceptions for special occasions. 'My friends stay out till midnight', they say. Oh yeah! 'No other parents insist on knowing where their children are.' Tell me another!

Action and consequence

PUNISHMENT OUTDATED?

The idea of punishment is outdated say some. What planet are they living on? The sooner a child gets used to the fact that actions have consequences the better. There are penalties on the road, penalties in the courts, penalties in business, penalties in school, penalties in sport; penalties are part of life. If the word penalty is preferred to punishment so be it, but punishment it is. Punishment has purpose; it is not just *to* the child, it is *for* the child.

Punishment is *for* the child

MEMO

- **Punishment is not discipline.** Punishment is *not* the same as discipline but *is* part of it. Punishment has to do with the past, what happened, discipline has to do with the present and the future, how to live. It is sometimes appropriate to show that you are angry, but the most significant thing is action, and confident action at that. Decisiveness shows you are in control, rage doesn't.

- **Punishment should fit the 'crime'.** A child needs to know that if he does 'this' then 'that' is the penalty. He knows what to expect and of course it should be proportionate to the 'crime'. You don't dock 1p from his pocket money if he throws a brick through your neighbour's window, nor do you ground her for six months for being five minutes late for a meal. If he acts badly and you are unsure what to do, it is worth giving yourself time to determine what your action should be, so that you don't act rashly in the heat of the moment.

○ **Punishment should be fair.** All too often parents take out their own problems on the kids, and that kind of 'undisciplined discipline' has more to do with the parents' feelings than their children's behaviour. If you are unfair they will respect you less and defy you more.

MEMO

If you are unfair they will respect you less and defy you more

Although you try to treat each child in a family the same, a sensitive co-operative child may have to be handled differently from her strong-willed brother. Getting the balance right is never easy.

- Punishment should be as soon after the event as possible so the child, especially a small one, knows what the connection is.
- Allowance should be made for childish irresponsibility, genuine mistakes or accidents.
- There may still have to be action and consequence but if there has not been wilful defiance you will deal with it differently.

KINDS OF CONSEQUENCES. Each child is unique and what is effective will vary from child to child. The consequences for misbehaviour should be known in advance.

○ **Verbal.** A stern look, a serious voice and a 'good talking to' is all that some children need. A thoughtful teenage girl reflected, 'The most effective disciplinary action Mum ever used was disappointment.' That was punishment enough for her.

○ **Cooling off.** Time out. Standing in a corner, facing a blank wall, being sent to their room, but *not* as happened to one, being locked in a cupboard. Some children of course like being sent to their room where they can do what they want. One eleven-year-old boy promptly climbed down the drainpipe into the garden. If there are stairs, a 'naughty step' is a good place to put a child, as there is nothing to do and there's time to think and cool down. Choose a safe place but a boring one. Some parents add one minute for each year of age.

o **Withdrawal of privileges.** The possibilities may range from docking pocket money, going to bed early, grounding, withdrawal of a treat, banning a favourite TV programme or access to computer, phone, mobile or car.

o **Confiscation.** If a toy causes an outbreak of hostilities or becomes a missile aimed at sibling or friend, then temporary deprivation will probably be at least part of the discipline.

> ... let them know it is their behaviour you disapproved of, not them
>
> MEMO

o **Physical.** A frustrated parent upset by constant crying might be tempted to shake a baby. Never, ever do so. It can result in serious brain damage.

What about smacking? Under fifteen to eighteen months a child is not capable of associating the event with the consequences. But some parents feel that if a child from say two to ten is wilfully and continuously defiant, or if there is danger, and if every other avenue of correction has been exhausted, then a short slap on the fingers may be appropriate. Others feel strongly that such action is never justified. The subject is highly sensitive, the debate ongoing, and the responsibility (as the law stands) is the parent's.

REASSURE AFTER CONFRONTATION. If there are tears after confrontation then hugs bring comfort and reassurance. But if the tears are prolonged or if there is an ongoing grouchy mood, be aware that the aim may be to punish the punisher! But when all is calm let them know it is their behaviour you disapproved of, not them. Your love is unchanged.

Developing character

D ^{1}2m

values and brainwashing; they follow your footsteps; values are caught; faith and integrity; sex and why wait; pressure of peers; TV and Internet; circle of friends

Developing character

If there is one thing you'll want to pass on to your children it's this – what you *are* is more important than what you *do*. Character must not be confused with personality. Personality is largely inborn, character is formed by choice. The one doesn't change significantly during life, the other can – for better or worse. Your genes are a key factor in their personality, so don't be too hard on the kids, they got them from you! Character is built by influence and choices, in the early years largely by your influence, as the years pass largely by their choices.

Character and values

EVERY PARENT IS A TEACHER

Every parent is a teacher. Good or bad, you teach; teach by what you say, teach by how you live. You have no option. Every child is a student. He listens and learns, she watches and copies. Long after the teacher is silent the marks remain. A woman said of her mother, 'She was my teacher though I didn't know I was being taught. I think she taught me as much by her tone of voice as by her words, and all these years later I remember not only what she said but the quiet confidence with which she said it. I learned to be a woman by watching her.'

MIND THE GAP. The really valuable things in life are not 'valuables' but values. What are yours? As rail passengers are warned to 'mind the gap' between train and platform, parents must ensure there is no gap between what they say and what they do. Values preached but not practised are not valued, for children identify more with behaviour than words. 'The footsteps a child follows,' someone wrote, 'are most likely to be the ones his parents thought they had covered up!' A boy of fifteen had lost so much respect for his father that when he heard that he had died, he said, 'I raced outside, rolling in the grass, squealing with delight.' Respect cannot be demanded, only earned, and they will respect your *values* more if they respect *you*.

Children identify more with behaviour than words

MEMO

Never pretend to be better than you are or excuse your mistakes or failure. What is *accused* in the daughter as temper should not be *excused* in the mother as nerves! If you insist your child says 'sorry', make sure they hear you say it.

HUGGED OR SLUGGED. If a child never knows whether he will be hugged or slugged or what contributes to the hugging or slugging, he loses respect for his parent. Then the lack of consistency leads to confusion as to what is actually right and wrong. In the best sense a parent needs to be predictable so the child is not at the mercy of parental moods.

ROLE MODEL. A debt collector came to the door of an impoverished home. When the mother realised who was at the door she told her son, 'Tell him I can't come, I'm in the bath.' The little boy went to the door and innocently announced, 'We ain't got no bath in this house, but my ma says she's in it!' Integrity is not learned by teaching a child to lie. Thoughtfulness is not taught by selfishness, nor respect by those who accuse and blame.

Parents not only model character they model marriage as well. If you show warmth and affection to your husband or wife in front of your children, they are likely to relate to their partners in the same way. When they see you disagree without being disagreeable they will hold that in their minds as long as they live. If you're kind and considerate to each other they will probably copy you. Your loyalty is a standard you set for your children. And of course the same applies to your parenting. Good points and bad they learn from you.

What children think of their father is affected by how their mother 'interprets' him. If she describes him as lazy and good-for-nothing that's how they'll see him. And the same goes for how he interprets his wife to them. The more you respect each other the more they will respect you. You may think they don't always listen, but be sure they always watch.

BRAINWASHING THE KIDS? Are you worried about brainwashing the kids by imposing your views and values on them? Don't be! Everybody else is trying to get to your children's brains, and every day their minds are bombarded by 'have this and be happy' advertisements. Your children are influenced by school, books, videos, DVDs, computers, music, magazines, films, radio, television and, above all, by friends. What they see, hear and experience is likely to shape their lives. If you have values worth holding you get there first!

MEMO

The overprotected child is under prepared for life

THE REAL WORLD. The real world is not an ideal world but don't protect them too much. The child whose knee was never scraped and whose ego was never bruised, is not prepared for the real world. Life is difficult and good does not always win. As much as a parent might want a garden of roses for a child, there will be a field of battle and he needs to be armed. He is armed best by the knowledge his parents give him, the values they instil, the standards they raise, the faith that shines through and the love that surrounds him.

Water is dangerous. Children can fall in and be drowned. So what do you do? Keep them away from it for the rest of their lives? No. You teach them to swim. The overprotected child is under prepared for life.

A good parent will monitor what the children watch and read and where they go. That's easy when they're small but when they are in their teens that's another story. If you don't allow them to watch a particular soap in the evening what happens at school next day? They feel right out of it. Parental protection leaves them unprotected from the values portrayed in the soap and from the scorn of their mates – 'Your mum didn't let you see it!' Most parents find that when they can no longer forbid they need to share. They make time to watch TV *with* their teens. Watching what they watch does three things. You know what your teens are seeing, the teens know that you know, and you can talk through some of the issues raised which would otherwise go unchallenged.

Character and faith

EVERY PARENT A TEACHER OF SPIRITUAL VALUES?

Yes, of course! You don't have to be an atheist to teach a child there is no God, you can live as if there were none. Besides, you teach by not teaching. Silence says, 'It's not important.'

Some say you shouldn't teach children about the Christian faith. They can 'decide for themselves' when they are older. On that basis atheists should not tell their children there is no God; they can work that out for themselves later on. Of course parents want to pass on to their children their values and beliefs. If they don't, it shows that they have none.

No privilege is greater or responsibility more awesome than teaching your child about God. There are five factors of paramount importance.

PERSONAL. Jesus did not ask people to become religious but said simply, 'Follow *me*', and the Gospels speak about those who 'received *him*.' Christianity is certainly a religion, but *being* a Christian is primarily a relationship with Christ. As the children absorbed *your* love, so live that they absorb *His*. But remember that 'you can no more tell what you don't know than you can come back from where you ain't been!' You can't give what you don't have.

MEMO

You can't give what you don't have

VISUAL. The two attributes of God that children most need to see in their parents are love and justice, and when they don't, there can be disturbing results. A woman cried, 'If God is anything like my father I could never trust Him,' and a man said quietly, 'If my mother is in heaven, I don't want to go there.' But when what is preached is practised you get the kind of tribute one man paid to his parents, 'From whose lips I first heard of Jesus and in whose lives I first saw Him.' For him their values were not just taught by what he heard, but 'caught' by what he saw.

NATURAL. It's good to establish a tradition of night-time prayers with the children, but if they are aware that you pray about all kinds of things at all kinds of times then praying will become natural to them. Don't let them grow up with a 'Sunday only' God mentality. If you are at ease in talking about spiritual things then they are more likely to be too.

COMMUNAL. Everyone knows that 'if you ever find a perfect church don't join it, for as soon as you join it, it will cease to be perfect'! Nonetheless it is important that you belong to a church for the Bible knows nothing of solitary Christianity.

- Go for a clearly Christ-centred church, for discipleship is far more important than denomination.
- Go to a church where there are young people and encourage your son or daughter to join in Christian clubs and camps.
- Don't *send* the children to church, *bring* them.
- Be fully involved but not to the extent that they feel that 'God has robbed me of my parents'.

PRACTICAL. It is well known that the Sea of Galilee is alive because it has both inflow and outflow. It gives away the water it receives. But the Dead Sea, which only has an inflow, gives nothing away and so is dead. The principle that you live as you give is never more true than in the Christian life. Set an example to your children of service to God and to others, and encourage them to do the same.

You live as you give

MEMO

If you take the Christian faith seriously you have probably prayed for your children since before they were born, and will do so as long as you live. But however much you might want your child to be a Christian the choice is his. The words in Proverbs 22:6, 'Train a child in the way he should go, and when he is old he will not turn from it', have been widely misunderstood. Proverbs is not a book of promises, but is what it says, a book of proverbs. Early training and example are immensely important and affect everything in the life of a child from physical health to spiritual life. But neither is guaranteed. In the story of the prodigal son the young man chose to turn his back on his father; he chose also to return. You and your children have free will.

Character and integrity

TRUTHFULNESS. If your children know that under no circumstances will you lie, it means not only that they will trust you absolutely but it sets a standard for them for the rest of their lives. Two men were studying documents about a situation which they had to investigate. On seeing the signature at the bottom of a letter, one man said to his friend, 'If George says it's true, then it's true.' End of story. That man's character was such that his word could not be doubted.

MONEY. Coming out of a shop with her small son a woman noticed that she had been given 50p too much change. She said, 'I must tell the man.' When she gave the money back the boy said, 'But Mum, if you hadn't given it back the man would never have known.' His mother answered, 'No, but I would!' Such small things make for high standards. When it comes to paying his taxes the boy-become-a-man will remember that shop door and his mother's words, 'I must tell.'

PROMISES. A father promised to fix his daughter's bicycle. He had just sat down to watch a match on TV when the girl said, 'Dad, I need my bike for tomorrow morning.' When he got up to do it she said, 'But Dad, you'll miss the football.' He laughed, 'My watching won't change the score, and besides I made a promise to you.' She'll remember that – a promise is a promise.

WORK. A teenage son was helping his father on a small building job. It soon became obvious to them both that the price the father had quoted and which had been accepted was inadequate. It would have been easy to cut a few corners but the son remembers his dad saying, 'No, this man is not going to suffer from my mistake. We'll do a good job.' Do a good job – that sticks.

Character and sex

HOW DID THE BABY GET IN? The best place to learn about sex is at home and the best teachers are parents. Polls consistently show that teenagers agree. The trouble is most parents are embarrassed by the unembarrassed enquiry, 'How did that baby get into Mummy's tummy?' A little boy wondered, 'is Mum like a washing-machine?' He had seen his mother put washing in and take it out, but was puzzled why a baby should take nine months to wash and spin.

BE OPEN ABOUT SEX. Give them facts appropriate to their age. Some children inconveniently don't ask questions but you can't afford to wait till puberty. It's far too late then. By that time they will have picked up more than you realise, and if you start a carefully rehearsed lecture in reproductive procedure *they* will be embarrassed. There are excellent books written for children of different ages which you can use to explain or amplify what you say. If you have talked with them at various times *before* puberty then it is much easier to talk when problems and pressures really arrive. Ignorance does not protect innocence; naivety is dangerous.

Ignorance does not protect innocence; naivety is dangerous

MEMO

It is important that they know about the changes in their bodies they can expect. For girls puberty usually begins between ten and thirteen years of age and for boys between eleven and fourteen. A thirteen-year-old girl committed suicide when, totally unprepared for the onset of menstruation, she thought she had a fatal illness. The clergyman who took the funeral service said, 'This must never happen again', and founded the confidential listening service known as the Samaritans.

BE POSITIVE ABOUT SEX. What you believe about sex will be reflected in what you say. Be positive about sex. It was God's idea and not invented by porn movie makers. Of human sexuality the Bible says, 'Male and female he created them', and then adds, 'God saw all that he had made, and it was very good' (Genesis 1:27,31). Your children need to know that sexual feelings are natural, normal and definitely OK.

BE CLEAR ABOUT MARRIAGE. The teaching of Jesus on marriage is clear (Matthew 19:3–6). It is sexual ('the two will become one flesh'), it is heterosexual ('male and female'), it is monogamous ('a man … his wife') and is meant to be permanent ('what God has joined together, let man not separate').

Whereas sexual feelings are definitely OK, many people believe, and this is the Christian standard, that sexual intercourse should be only for marriage. For a married person to have sex with someone other than their husband or wife is adultery, a legal as well as biblical term. The Bible also teaches that sexual immorality is not confined to adultery but includes other sexual practices outside marriage (see 1 Corinthians 6:9–10). There are tremendous pressures on individuals and couples in today's world, but for a Christian the standard is faithfulness in marriage and abstinence outside it.

BOYFRIEND/GIRLFRIEND. This is a tough one for parent and child.

o **Groups.** When girls and boys are in groups the interaction helps them to understand the opposite sex without the pressures of pairing off.

o **Age.** Few young people are sufficiently mature to handle a girl–boy relationship until the later teens. Talk it through with them, long before they get there, so they know what your expectations are.

o **Time.** With school and other commitments, a friendship is best when spaced and parents have to exercise responsibility here. One teenage girl said after an intense friendship ended, 'I wish we had rationed the time we spent together.'

o **Touch.** It's been said that the best rule of thumb is not to touch 'any part of the other person that you yourself don't have!'

o **Parents.** A parent's job is to support and protect, and it's very important that they get to know the girl or boy their son or daughter is going out with. A boy is more likely to treat his girlfriend with respect if he knows there is a parent or parents he has to face.

WHY WAIT? Behind the standard there are strong reasons. Your young people *will* come under pressure, perhaps sooner than you think, and it will help them keep standards if they have reasons. So many have said they didn't know how to say 'no' or even why. Here are some reasons:

o **Experience.** There does *not* need to be prior sexual experience to have a good marriage. In fact men and women who marry as virgins usually have fewer sexual problems and more lasting marriages. They learn together without bad memories and emotional baggage from the past. They reckon that good sex, with its ingredients of respect, commitment and loyalty, is worth waiting for.

o **Sexually transmitted infections.** These are widespread and have consequences ranging from pain and infertility to death. HIV is the virus which results in AIDS, the disease which spans the world and has killed millions. Condoms, properly used, help prevent STIs, but completely 'safe sex' does not exist.

o **Pregnancy.** Teenagers should be aware of the different methods of contraception, and also that none is 100 per cent safe. Condoms, particularly when used by young people, are no guarantee against pregnancy, and unwanted pregnancies have no easy answers. A girl who had an abortion said, 'At the time it seemed "sensible", but I can never look at a baby now without feeling that I took away a life.' A woman who had her child adopted cried, 'There has never been one day in thirty-four years that I have not thought of her.' A girl struggling terribly as a lone parent, summed it up with, 'I love my child, but sometimes I feel so stupid … five minutes doing it … fifteen years regretting it.'

MEMO

A moment of madness … a lifetime of regret

o **Casual sex.** Water is good, but in the very water in which you swim you can also drown. Sex in itself is good and healthy but misused is enormously destructive. It would be foolish to say there is no pleasure in casual sex. Of course there is; that's why it happens. But there are consequences other than pregnancy or sexual infections. Here is what some found.

- Self-esteem. A girl said, 'The only thing my boyfriend wants me for is sex. I feel used and dirty.' A man confessed, 'I despise the girls who let me do it, and despise myself.'
- Confusion. 'I don't know whether this is love or lust.'
- Meaning. A teenage boy said, 'I could have it whenever I wanted and it no longer has any meaning. I'm sick of sex.'
- Regret. A third of girls say, 'I was drunk at the time.' An older man reflected, 'It was a moment of madness for which I've had a lifetime of regret.'

- **Cohabitation.** Cohabitation breaks down four to five times more often than marriage, and even when a cohabiting couple marry each other that marriage is twice as likely to break down.

PRESSURE POINTS

- **Peer pressure.** 'Everybody does it.' If everyone stole and lied it wouldn't make stealing or lying right, but it is simply not true that everyone has sex outside marriage. Not everything teenagers boast of actually happens! The answer a girl might give to the old line, 'If you love me you will', might be, 'if you love me you won't. Stop pressuring me.'

- **Television.** Television doesn't affect behaviour? Tell that to the advertising companies! Of course it does; of course your young people are affected by what they see. When they are small you are a not-so-remote TV controller, but as they get bigger the most you can hope to be is a TV guide. Have television in the family space in your home rather than your children's bedrooms. You can have standards about what videos, DVDs and computer games are used in your home but you have no control over what they see elsewhere. If you try to enforce total control, their resentment against you will be even more damaging than what they watch.

  But you can make a difference. If you are dissatisfied with the amount of sex and violence on TV say so, not just *about* the TV companies but *to* them. If there are good programmes say so. Your praise and protest *does* make a difference.

- **The Internet.** A few clicks and both your home and your children's minds are invaded by pornography. They will see things they will *never* be able to forget. Don't think, 'Oh my children wouldn't look at stuff like that.' Yes, they would. They are children and are naturally curious. What will they see? Sex? Yes, heterosexual sex, homosexual sex, group sex, sex with children, sex with animals. They may be shocked at first but can be hooked. Their minds will be polluted by the sexual images, so it is vital to install a filter on your computer. If you don't know how to download it, get someone to do it for you. There's a charge for a filter, but if it blocks the images which would corrupt your child, it's cheap at the price.

Character and friends

FIRST FRIENDS. The first friends your child makes are very significant. She learns to play, to share and to stand up for herself. Often her friends are the children of your friends who likely share at least some of your values, so she learns what language and behaviour are acceptable.

TEEN SCENE. It's friends before family. Teenagers are both rebels and conformists; rebels against the status quo and conformists with their peers. They fall into line on dress, hairstyle, music, words and activities. It is so enormously important to be accepted by their friends that you may actually feel redundant. Parents, hanging on every word that psychologist Dr James Dobson said about the teen years, heard him say, 'This is what I recommend. Get them through it!'

YOUR ATTITUDE. Ask questions about their friends. 'Why do you like her … what do you most enjoy when you hang out with them?' Never dismiss or rubbish them. There may be times you really see a danger they can't see, and then you have a right (and responsibility) to speak out. But do all you can to make their friends welcome in your home. Make your home a fun place to come to. Your children will be grateful to you for respecting their friends.

SAYING 'NO'. Every child and teenager will be put under pressure to go somewhere they don't want to go, or do something they don't want to do or feel is wrong. Let them know that you don't have to say 'yes' to be liked. The word 'no' may actually bring greater respect than 'yes'. They can be up front with, 'No thanks, I don't want to …' or 'No, I've got to …', and if they are not sure, they can play for time with, 'I'll have to check …' Another response is, 'Not this time, but thanks for asking me.' The rule in saying 'no' is to be pleasant but firm, but if the pressure is (say) to do drugs then they can drop the courtesy with, 'No way!' and turn on their heel.

You don't have to say 'yes' to be liked

MEMO

BEING DIFFERENT. That comes naturally to some. One young man laughed, 'It's not that I want to be different; I just don't want to be the same!' Encourage your child to stand up for what is right, to stand out from the crowd if necessary, to take a lead in interesting and fun things. When he does, let him know you are proud of him.

Character and choice

DEVELOPING CHARACTER. A student spoke profoundly when she said, 'All my life I have blamed my father for what I am, but now I realise that I am responsible for me.'

The development of your children's character starts with you and your influence, but in the end is their choice. Character is the product of habits they have consciously or unconsciously formed, and there are no instant habits. Character takes time and good character practice.

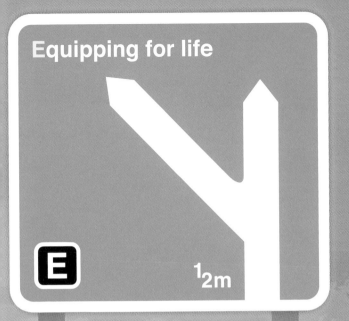

Equipping for life

E ^{1}2m

learning social skills; manners and money; keeping them safe; accidents at home; safe on the roads; protect from abuse; towards healthy bodies

Equipping for life

A journey into uncharted territory, either on earth or in space, will not go better than its preparation. Life is a journey and the child setting out for a mysterious world needs the best of preparation and equipment. Your son or daughter will encounter many testing situations from which you cannot protect them, but for which you can prepare them.

Social skills

Put a new piece of software into a computer and instantly the information is there. The computer doesn't forget and will always do what you say (in theory anyway). But children aren't computers, they are sponges, and they soak up information randomly, mostly from parents.

Many adults feel embarrassed or inadequate because they do not have abilities they see in friends or workmates. They may be laughed at, lose out on job opportunities, or find that a longed-for friendship never develops, because they do not have basic social skills. What are those skills?

GOOD MANNERS. Good manners are basically showing consideration for others.

o **Mealtimes.** There are times when it is OK to eat with fingers, but every child needs to know how to use knife, fork and spoon in a restaurant or someone else's house, and they learn mealtime manners best at home. The basics are sitting rather than slouching, not starting before everyone else or talking with their mouth full, asking for something to be passed rather than reach-and-grab, and not leaving the table without asking. When they ask let them go. Few five-year-olds are turned on by discussion of international politics.

o **Writing.** Help your child develop an attitude of gratitude by getting them to write 'thank you' notes promptly, and make sure they can write business letters. A young man of eighteen hadn't a clue how to write one and ended a letter to his bank manager with the words, 'with love from'. The manager, unaccustomed to such expressions of affection from clients, probably had the letter framed.

o **Conversation.** You want your kids to relate well to people as they grow up? Then let them learn the most important words in the English language – please, thank you, sorry, excuse me, hello and goodbye. How long do they take to say? One second. Yet those words can change the quality and direction of your child's life.

Is there a code of conduct in conversation? Yes. Look at the person while they are talking … avoid interrupting … swallow yawns … never ridicule … respond with something more than 'yeah' … learn to ask questions and be interested in other people. One of the best ways of teaching children to eat and talk properly is around the table at home. One of the good memories many children have is sitting at table talking, listening, arguing, laughing. It prepares them for life better than a TV dinner. Have family meals as often as possible.

o **Language.** Exactly what constitutes 'bad language' is not easily defined, but words that make light of religion or describe certain bodily functions are part of it. Many parents have zero tolerance for the words God or Jesus Christ being used as swear words, and for the F & B words because they are offensive and usually totally irrelevant. Few actually gain respect by using bad language and no one loses respect by not using it.

o **Mobiles.** Make a mobile a servant not a master. It should be switched off during public gatherings. It's wrong that a wedding, funeral, church service, film, class or concert should be interrupted by a mobile. To this list should be added family mealtimes.

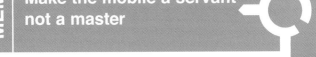

MEMO

Make the mobile a servant not a master

MONEY. Your children won't handle life well if they can't handle money. Talk to them about what is –

o **Allowed.** You may discreetly check with other parents to see the going rate for pocket money or allowance and then decide the level for your children. These will need to be adjusted upwards as they get older. And don't forget inflation (as if you could!).

o **Earned.** They shouldn't be paid for every household chore they do, for they need to learn 'if you use it look after it', but if they want to earn extra cash there could be some jobs for which they are paid. As they get up into their teens they may have part-time jobs outside their home, where they earn a wage, learn about time-keeping and working with others.

o **Saved.** From the beginning encourage them to save, whether it comes from pocket money or from what they earn. The amounts may be small but the habit is huge.

o **Spent.** Sometimes they may, in your judgment, waste their money, but don't rush to stop them unless it's something serious. They must learn from mistakes. Later on they'll have to learn about borrowing (student fees, mortgages etc) but in the early years most parents discourage their children from buying what they can't afford. They value more the things they wait for. You want to avoid the 'want it, get it' attitude. If they overspend, be careful about bailing them out. It can become an expectation.

They value more the things they wait for

MEMO

○ **Given.** There's a happy medium between the Scrooge who gives nothing and the generous soul who would give away every penny. Learning to buy presents is important and so is giving to church or charity.

○ **Managed.** Depending on age and stage teach them to keep account of what comes in and what goes out. How to stick to a budget and handle a cheque book and credit card are life lessons of careful management. Built into their psyche it can save headache and heartbreak.

CLOTHES

○ **Shopping.** It's a graduated experience from when you do all the choosing, to teaching them the reasons for your choices, to their learning to choose with you, until finally they choose without you. Not just size and style and colour but quality, ease of maintenance and how it fits with other clothes. Bring them shopping with you (some will love it, some hate it) until they have an understanding of products and prices. Ask, 'What do *you* think is the best, and why?' You might even ask your teenagers to help you with your choices.

○ **Storage.** Encourage them into a routine of hanging and folding. If there are clothes which can't be passed to friends or younger siblings, give away what isn't used. There are people out there who would be only too glad to put on what they cast off.

o **Washing and ironing.** How will they learn if they don't *do* it? They won't do the ironing as well or as quickly as you, but get them to do it sometimes.

KEEPING CLEAN. A fine young man asked, 'When I meet a girl, within minutes she's gone. What's wrong with me?' When someone told him frankly it was his BO he was amazed. He had had no training in personal hygiene and was totally unconscious of it. A regular bath or shower and change of clothing are not only healthy for both sexes but a social must.

COOKING. Gone are the days when a man, after his wife died, discovered at eighty that you boil water to make tea. Be sure your children know the basics of food shopping, preparation and cooking. Don't send them into the world with zero knowledge of hob, oven and microwave. Start early, overlook the mess and eat their failures!

MEMO

Overlook the mess and eat their failures!

SWIMMING. Learning to swim may save your child's life, but swimming is also a social skill which can be shared with friends and influence holidays.

DRIVING. A girl qualified fully as a social worker but couldn't get the job she wanted because she couldn't drive. To know how to drive and to drive safely is an important social skill.

Keeping them safe

ACCIDENTS AT HOME

○ **Accidents will happen.** About half of all deaths of children under five in the UK happen at home, and over one million children under fifteen land in hospital for accidents which occur in and around home. Most accidents are preventable.

○ **Think the unthinkable.** Use fireguards, stair gates and socket covers (ever seen a toddler trying to slip a key into a power socket?), child-resistant window locks and cupboards, coiled or cordless kettles. If there are small children around use the rear hot plates of the cooker, with pan handles turned in. Have medicine cupboards locked and toxic or sharp items out of reach. Protect glass doors and tables with safety glass film, and make sure heaters and shelves are securely anchored so they can't fall over. A dragged tablecloth can produce more than interesting sound effects.

Sleep babies on their backs and never have them in a high chair without a harness. Take care with water; a small child can drown in a couple of inches. Cats have curled up on the face of a baby. A four-year-old boy climbed on a chair, put his head through the pull cord of a Venetian blind, and fell off. He was dead when his mother came into the room. Think the unthinkable.

○ **Take a first aid course.** If your child was choking or had stopped breathing would you know what to do? Why not take a first aid course?

FIRE! FIRE!

○ **Smoke alarms.** A man put a smoke alarm outside the kitchen and then disconnected the battery because the alarm kept going off. He lost his entire family. Properly fitted and maintained smoke alarms will *halve* the risk of you and your children being killed in a fire.

o **Kitchen care.** Nearly two-thirds of all fires start in the kitchen. Be especially careful when cooking with hot oils. Have a fire blanket handy so that in seconds you can smother a fire.

o **Escape route.** Think ahead; what's your escape route? Plan it, then practise it. If the alarm goes off at 3.00am you don't have to think because you have already thought. You know and the children know. Brief the babysitter. If there are locked doors, make sure you and the children and the babysitter know where the keys are.

o **Close doors.** Some like sleeping with their bedroom door open either for ventilation or to hear if a child cries. But always close doors downstairs because fire and smoke go upwards.

o **Gas and electricity.** If you have gas have the unit serviced annually by a qualified engineer. That's better than losing a child to fumes from a faulty appliance. Don't overload sockets and extensions. If in doubt check with someone suitably qualified.

o **Tips about bits.** If you use cigarettes stub them out carefully. An ash tray in the shape of a skull had printed on it, 'Poor Uncle Fred, he smoked in bed'! Many a home has been destroyed when a candle used for emergency lighting was not properly secured. Put matches and lighters out of reach. Children trust you unthinkingly; don't let them down. Be sure, be safe; their lives are in your hands.

ACCIDENTS ON THE ROADS

- **Crossing roads.** Small children have difficulty in judging speed and distance. Teach the Green Cross Code – think first, stop, use your eyes and ears, wait until it's safe to cross, look and listen, arrive alive. Children are not ready to cross roads on their own before they are about eight. Teach the Code by doing it yourself.

- **Cycling.** Properly fitting helmets (try before you buy) save head injuries. At night a bicycle must have a white light in front, a back red light and a red reflector. In addition it is sensible to use reflective clothing. A cycling proficiency course may save limbs and lives.

- **Seat belts.** At 30 mph an unrestrained person can be thrown forward with a force of 30 to 60 times their own body weight. All children under 135 centimetres (4' 5") in height MUST have the correct child restraint and it MUST be properly fitted. The *driver* is responsible for seeing that under fourteens in the car are wearing safety belts.

No risks on the road

MEMO

- **Driving.** Let your young people know loud and clear – *never ever drink and drive*. Life in a wheelchair is not funny. If they are responsible for an accident when they are driving and their friend in the car is killed, how are they going to explain that to her parents? A single drink could mean one accident and four funerals. Get it deep into their brain – *heed your speed*. It's not clever, it's not cool to break speed limits. Far more can be lost than losing their licence. They should refuse to be driven by someone they believe has been drinking. Remind them also that to drive while using a handheld phone is illegal, and can be as dangerous as driving over the limit with alcohol. Get it deep into their brain – no risks on the road.

Sexual abuse

YOUR OWN RELATIONSHIP. If they feel close to you and enjoy physical contact with you as a parent, they will find it easier to distinguish between good touch and what is 'yucky'. If you always listen to them they will be much more likely to tell you if there's some person they feel uncomfortable with, or about a situation which scares them.

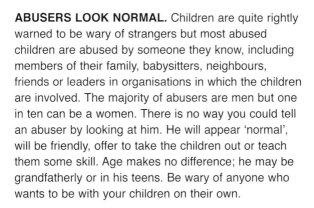

MEMO

'My body's nobody's body but mine. You mind your own body; let me mind mine.'

ABUSERS LOOK NORMAL. Children are quite rightly warned to be wary of strangers but most abused children are abused by someone they know, including members of their family, babysitters, neighbours, friends or leaders in organisations in which the children are involved. The majority of abusers are men but one in ten can be a women. There is no way you could tell an abuser by looking at him. He will appear 'normal', will be friendly, offer to take the children out or teach them some skill. Age makes no difference; he may be grandfatherly or in his teens. Be wary of anyone who wants to be with your children on their own.

WARNING WITHOUT ALARMING

o **It's OK to say 'no'.** The parts of the body which are covered by swimwear are private (buttocks, anus, genitals and breasts). The mouth (because some sexual abuse is oral) is for food and drink, medicine if need be, and a toothbrush! Of course sometimes the doctor or dentist may have to look into it. There's a catchy song, 'My body's nobody's body but mine. You mind your own body; let me mind mine.'

Children have a right to eat, drink, sleep, go to the toilet, and a right not to be touched, or be made to touch, in ways that frighten them or they don't like. If someone tries to lift their skirt or put a hand down their trousers, it's OK to say 'no'. It's right, not rude! Kidscape have a good rule 'Yell, Run, Tell', and it's good to practise it, perhaps in front of a mirror, so they are not shy about doing it. Then in a real emergency they can do it instinctively.

○ **Encourage them to tell.** An abuser will often say, 'Don't tell anyone. If you do, I'll …' and he will make threats against the child or those the child loves. He may add, 'Anyway, nobody will believe you.' Make sure your child knows that if a person speaks like this he is lying, and the one thing they *must* do is to tell. There are 'good secrets' about birthday presents, Christmas gifts and special surprises, but if anyone touches them in a way they don't like and they are asked not to tell, then that's *definitely* a 'bad secret' and they *should* tell.

Play 'what if …' games. These are good ways of warning without alarming. 'What if you smelled smoke downstairs, what would you do?' 'What if our dog ran across the road in front of a car, what would you do?' 'What if a car pulled up beside you while you were walking and a man asked you the way, what would you do?'

STREET PROOF YOUR CHILD. They have to spread their wings so give them strategies to keep them safe. Of course a lot depends on the age of your child and where you live, but here are some guidelines.

- **Safety in numbers.** Walk with a friend or in a group whenever possible. On a train sit in a carriage where there are other people.

- **Keep your distance.** It's OK to ignore someone who asks for directions in the street or from a car. Don't take lifts from people you don't know.

- **Public toilets.** Go into the toilet area or washroom with a friend if possible. If you are on your own and anyone talks to you or touches you, don't answer, just walk out quickly. Never go into a cubicle with anyone no matter what they say.

- **Don't take it.** Don't take sweets, money or presents of any kind from people you don't know, even if they say they know your Mum or Dad.

- **Emergencies.** Make sure they know how to make an emergency 999 call and how they can contact you if they need to.

- **Avoid lonely areas.** Avoid unlit or isolated places and be careful of short cuts down back alleys or lonely lanes.

- **Pre-arrange** how and when they will get home and with whom.

- **In case of delay.** If you have arranged to meet your child at a certain time and place, have a backup plan in case you or they are delayed. Don't depend entirely on mobiles for they can be lost, stolen or need recharging.

- **Chat rooms.** Chat rooms can be fun but are inherently dangerous. A 14-year-old girl thought she had met a nice boy and didn't know a 44-year-old paedophile was grooming her for sex. Have an absolute rule that your child must *never* meet *anyone* they have been in touch with over the Internet, without your knowledge and approval. Make sure they *never* divulge their name, address, telephone number or password. To do so is like giving a key of the house to a stranger.

Towards healthy bodies

Your lifestyle influences your child's health more than anything else, and if you get it wrong it can take ten to fifteen years off your life – and theirs.

EATING. Children are affected by the eating habits of parents. They eat mostly what you eat because that's what you provide. Poor diet leads to more colds and infections, bad teeth and gums, poor concentration at school, anaemia, obesity, and later to coronary heart disease, high blood pressure, bowel cancer, diabetes and osteoporosis.

'The healthy way of five a day' is well established, for fruit and vegetables are low in calories and have fibre and nutrients that reduce the risk of chronic diseases. Go easy on salt, sugar, alcohol and caffeine, and opt for whole grain cereals and breads, low-fat milk, lean meat and poultry. Encourage mineral water and fruit juices rather than sugary drinks, and snacking on fruit rather than crisps and sweets. Side effects of a good diet are glossier hair, stronger nails, clearer skin, and more energy. In getting your children to widen the range of what they eat, be wise and introduce one new food at a time.

EXERCISE. Lack of exercise has effects similar to poor diet but regular exercise is not only mood improving and weight reducing but also helps the machinery of the body to run well. With exercise the body produces endorphins which are natural 'feel-good' chemicals which lift the mood, improve sleep and maintain appetite. Those who exercise regularly are more likely to feel well and stay well, and are less likely to be involved in destructive habits.

DRUGS, TOBACCO AND ALCOHOL
(SEE PAGES 94–101)

HYGIENE. Build into their psyche that they *always* wash their hands after going to the toilet. It is not realistic to get a child to wash her hands before every snack, but the old 'wash hands before meals' is a good habit. A regular bath or shower and the brushing of teeth morning and night are healthy practices with obvious social benefits.

Facing big issues

F   1/2m

beating the bully; dealing with drugs;
divorce and the family; single parents; no
'steps' in the house; parents in pain; what's
to be done?

Some parents seem to face all the issues but all parents face some. It's a tough world out there for both parent and child and it leaves you wondering how on earth you are going to manage.

Bullying

WHAT HAPPENS? Bullying includes being teased, called names, pushed, pulled, pinched, hit, kicked, having their bag, money, mobile or other possessions taken or thrown around. They may be ridiculed, ignored or excluded from a group, having rumours spread about them or receiving abusive texts or emails. The emotional bullying is often harder to cope with than physical. Cyber-bullying including happy-slapping is a serious extension of bullying.

WHO DOES IT? Bullies usually have problems of their own and it is widely recognised that hurt people hurt people. Some merely want to show off or seem tougher than they are. For others it is a power game, and intimidating those who seem smaller or weaker makes them feel bigger and stronger.

WHAT EFFECT DOES IT HAVE? Even a one-off incident hurts, but when it is continued it is devastating. A child feels anxious, fearful, depressed, humiliated – and powerless to stop it. A girl said, 'I wake up in the morning with a sick feeling in my stomach as I think of what's going to happen today.' Academic levels may plunge. Some develop mysterious headaches or tummy aches and don't want to go to school. They can feel there is something wrong with *them* or even that it is *their* fault that they are being bullied. Depression can set in and a few find it so unbearable they attempt suicide. The effects of bullying can last a lifetime.

WHAT CAN A PARENT DO? Do something! Don't let them suffer in silence.

- Be alert for tell-tale scratches or bruises, trouble with doing schoolwork, missing possessions, acting out of character or taking a different route to or from home.
- Listen carefully and caringly to what they say. You need to know what's happening and they need to know you care.
- Be very slow to brush it aside with 'it's just a bit of teasing' and 'it's part of growing up', or dismiss it with 'sort it out yourself'. They're probably telling you because they can't. And that's not easy to admit.
- If this is more than a one-off then keep a log of what happens, when and where the incidents have been, and who is involved.
- Approach the school if that is where the bullying happens. Most schools have a bullying policy and it is in their own interests to do something about it.
- Make sure your home is a happy place to be, with plenty of love and fun.
- Don't stop till the bullying stops.

Illegal drugs

Curiosity, boredom, rebelliousness, the wish to seem adult or escape from problems, the pressure of mates and 'it feels good', all combine to draw young people into drugs. They see a bit of powder, a small pill or capsule, what looks like a tiny piece of paper with a picture on it, and think there's nothing to worry about. The road in is quick and easy, the road out can be long and hard, and some never make it. No supplier cares a jot about what happens to your teenagers. The drug baron smiles and grows fat on your child's misery. The only thing the 'friendly' dealer wants is to make friends with your child's money. Make sure your kids are:

WELL INFORMED. The three main *groups* of illegal drugs are:

- Depressants (downers) which slow down bodily processes and make a person less aware (cannabis and opiates like heroin).
- Stimulants (uppers) which raise levels of activity in the body and make a person feel more alert and energetic (cocaine, crack, ecstasy, amphetamines like speed).
- Hallucinogens (psychedelics) which distort the senses and perceptions (LSD, magic mushrooms). Cannabis may have hallucinogenic effects as well as depressant.

> **MEMO** The road into drugs is quick and easy, the road out can be long and hard

The three main *classes* of illegal drugs are:
- Class A Heroin, LSD, ecstasy, cocaine, crack, magic mushrooms
- Class B Amphetamines like speed, barbiturates etc
- Class C Cannabis, anabolic steroids, ketamine, GHB etc

Consequences
- Penalties. Supply or even possession of *any* drug in *any* of these classes can attract fines or imprisonment or both. This includes cannabis. In the case of Class A drugs, possession has a maximum penalty of seven years' imprisonment and supply up to fourteen years.
- Driving. The penalties for driving under the influence of drugs are the same as driving under

the influence of alcohol.

- Job opportunities. A criminal conviction may hinder job opportunities.
- Manufacture. As there is no control over manufacture, a drug may be stronger than the last time it was tried, so the effects may be greater than intended.
- Mixing drugs. Two drugs mixed together or with alcohol can be extremely dangerous.
- Negative effects. Negative effects include impaired judgment, loss of memory and co-ordination, breathing problems, blurred vision, seizures and death. Drugs like GHB and Rohypnol can cause unconsciousness with users unable to remember anything that happened while under the influence of the drug. Long-term effects include cancers, heart problems and kidney failures.
- Sharing needles or syringes risks HIV/AIDS and Hepatitis B and C.
- Addiction. If the drug forms a habit then the habit needs money, and the need for money may mean violence and theft, which in turn may mean prison.

○ **Signs of drug use.** There is an unpredictability about most teenagers but a combination of some of the following may indicate a growing drug habit – changes in sleep pattern, appetite, life cycle, moods or friends. To these can be added poor memory, lethargy, lack of interest in normal activities, decreased school performance, lack of personal hygiene, coarsening of features, and shortage or disappearance of money.

○ **Calmly confident.** It's OK to say 'no'. Let your teenagers know that far from losing respect they will gain it for having the courage to refuse. The great majority of young people don't do drugs. One teenager when pressured laughed confidently, 'No way. I may not have much of a brain but I am going to look after the one I have.' Another answered, 'Open-minded? That's why I said "no". I want a mind to be open-minded with!'

Legal drugs

TOBACCO. There is no law against smoking cigarettes but it is illegal for shops to sell them to anyone under sixteen. Tobacco advertisements are banned in the UK from TV, billboards, magazines, newspapers and websites. Nicotine is a highly addictive drug and few people are occasional smokers. Smokers are quickly hooked and surveys show that over 80 per cent of teenagers who smoke become addicted. Apart from the short-term effects ('kiss a non-smoker and taste the difference!') the dangers of smoking, because they are long-term, are difficult for young people to appreciate. The following are some of the effects of smoking cigarettes.

- **Cancers galore.** Smokers are more likely to get pneumonia, emphysema and chronic bronchitis, strokes, heart attacks, coronary disease and *many* cancers. Lung cancer is about nine times more common in smokers than non-smokers.

- **From wrinkles to impotence.** Premature wrinkling of the skin is more likely with smokers, who also have a higher risk of blindness, infertility in women and impotence in men.

- **From croup to cot death.** If a mother continues to smoke during the first year of her baby's life the child is more likely to get croup, pneumonia, bronchitis or meningitis. Cot deaths are more common where there are smoking mothers.

- **Smoked to death.** The 'Smoking kills' printed on cigarette packets is literally true, for between a third and a half of people who smoke for a lifetime will eventually have a smoking-related death.

- **Money to burn.** Two twenty-a-day smokers will in their lifetime smoke approximately the value of an average-priced home in the United Kingdom.

ALCOHOL. Few parents like their children to do drugs in any form, but kids say, 'But Mum, Dad, you drink and smoke and what's the difference?' Although alcohol is widely used socially and undoubtedly gives a buzz and sense of well being, that must be balanced by the fact that it *is* an addictive drug. Tolerance increases with use, dependence can creep up and vulnerability varies from person to person. A report from the World Health Organisation identifies alcohol as the third highest risk to health in developed countries. Young people need to be aware of the dangers of alcohol and your example as parents can be a major factor in shaping your children's attitude.

Although the possession or use of alcohol is not in itself illegal, it is for anyone under eighteen to buy it from a pub, off-licence or supermarket. The Department of Health advises that men should not drink more than three to four units of alcohol per day, and women no more than two to three units per day (1 pint of ordinary strength beer or glass of wine = 2 units, 1 alcopop = 1.5 units, 1 pub measure of spirits = 1 unit). There is of course no 'safe level' of alcohol, for a single glass can begin a habit which spirals out of control.

Binge dinking is difficult to define, but the British Medical Association concludes that it 'usually refers to heavy drinking over an evening or similar time span'. It is often in groups and with the intention of becoming drunk. It is very dangerous. The long-term health effects of alcohol abuse such as heart disease, strokes, many cancers, cirrhosis of the liver, alcoholic poisoning and mental health problems are well documented, but the following are some of the more immediate negative effects that parents and young people should know.

○ **Young adults.** Alcohol-related deaths are the most common cause of death in young adults.

○ **Violence.** Alcohol contributes to more than 40 per cent of violent crime and 80 per cent of criminal damage.

- **Driving deaths.** One in six drivers killed in road accidents have drunk more than the legal limit for driving which is 80 milligrams of alcohol in 100 millilitres of blood. If a person is found guilty of causing death by dangerous driving they can spend many years in prison. Do not drink and drive.

- **Accident and Emergency.** About 30 per cent of admissions to hospital A & Es are alcohol related.

- **Pregnancy.** When a woman drinks alcohol during pregnancy it passes to the baby through the umbilical cord, and that can result in a child having problems ranging from learning disabilities to physical abnormalities.

- **Sexual infections.** Young people are *many times* less likely to use condoms regularly where there is a pattern of alcohol and sex, thus greatly increasing unwanted pregnancies and sexual infections.

- **Family.** Alcohol is a factor in a third of domestic violence incidents, and its misuse by parents identified in 50 per cent of child protection cases. Marriages are twice as likely to end in divorce where there are alcohol problems.

- **Black coffee.** The only thing that helps the body process alcohol is time; a bucketful of black coffee won't do it.

A young man took a risk after a party and drove home under the influence of alcohol. He said afterwards, 'It was the stupidest thing I ever did. I lost my licence, and then because I couldn't drive I lost my job, and when I lost my job there were so many rows at home I lost my marriage. Now I hardly ever see my children. And all because of a couple of extra drinks. Stupid, stupid, stupid!'

SOLVENTS. Solvents are substances whose fumes are breathed to get a cheap 'high'. Glues, aerosols, petrol and cigarette lighter refills are among the most common, and most of the sniffing is done by young people in groups. It can lead to heart failure or to choking to death on vomit. Most sniffers move on to alcohol or other drugs when they have the money.

WHAT CAN A PARENT DO?

What do you do if you think your child is using drugs, illegal or legal?

○ **Be calm.** You may not feel calm but if you overreact they are more likely to be defensive. Talk it over with them when *you* are not angry and when *they* are not intoxicated or under the influence of drugs.

○ **Be clear.** Quietly try to get the facts – what drug or drink, how much, how often, when and where. Listen to them. Do your best to understand. Your attitude will help their openness.

○ **Be firm.** If they are under eighteen you have a responsibility and there are times that love must be tough. If you are fair you don't need to worry about being firm. The day may come when they will say with one young man, 'I'm glad you stood up to me. If you hadn't, I don't know where I would be today. Thanks!'

○ **Be reassuring.** Assure them it's the drug you don't like, or the way they are using alcohol, but that you love *them*. She's your daughter, he's your son. Nothing, absolutely nothing, will change that.

○ **Be strong.** How do they feel? Rebellious, confused, defensive? Probably all those things. But along with that, there may be guilt or embarrassment or fear. Let them know you are there for them, for although they may not say it, they need you to be strong.

Don't hesitate to get help for them and for yourself, from friends or the church or from professionals in the area of drugs or alcohol.

○ **Be patient.** The problem may be quickly dealt with, but if not, then remember some of the greatest words ever written, 'Love is patient, love is kind … it keeps no record of wrongs … always hopes, always perseveres' (1 Corinthians 13:4–7). Do your best to live that love.

Divorce

EFFECTS OF BREAKDOWN OF MARRIAGE

When it comes to children, the old maxim 'a good divorce is better than a bad marriage' is very misleading. Sometimes there is of course no alternative to divorce but all the evidence is that the break-up of the home *severely* impacts children, and the effects are long-lasting. Children who come from a broken home are more likely to divorce if they marry and break up if they cohabit, to perform less well at school, to be physically or sexually abused, to have drug and alcohol addictions, and psychological and emotional problems.

Though these things are statistically *more likely* to occur with the children of broken homes, clearly they *do not necessarily follow*, and there are many wonderful examples of those who beat the stats. But these are facts and should be taken into account when decisions are made which will affect children.

COPING WITH DIVORCE OR SEPARATION

When parents part there are almost always emotions in which the children are caught up. The degree to which they are affected is greatly influenced by the ongoing attitude of the parents to each other. At best it is rarely simple. The absent parent may lavish presents and holidays on a child, while the resident parent has to cope with the mundane. Children can try to play one parent off against the other.

HOW DO YOU COPE?

o **Expect erratic behaviour** from the children; you'll get it. Tearful, moody, aggressive, clingy, rebellious, they may withdraw into dreaming, find difficulty in concentrating, or lose interest, at least for a time, in things they had liked most.

o **Reassure them** that it is *not* their fault, for it is very common for children (particularly younger ones) to feel *they* are in some way to blame. Tell them over and over again that you love them, and spend as much time with them as possible.

o **Encourage them** to maintain a relationship with their other parent and avoid making negative comments whatever your own feelings may be. Bite your tongue. When the children are older if they don't want to visit the absent parent you can't make them.

o **Listen to them** if they want to tell you about what they do with the other parent, but don't pump for information.

o **Discuss any problems** with the other parent as amicably as possible. If the courts have not defined access you may have to compromise. Arrange pick-up and drop-off points. Talk calmly in a business-like manner but not in the presence of the children. Put what you have agreed in writing and carry out what you have undertaken.

o **Explain decisions** to the children for fear of the unknown is hard for them to handle. They need to know what to expect.

- **Never use the children** as ammunition to get at the other parent.

- **Maintain routines** as far as possible in other areas of their lives.

  Note: if there are real concerns about the safety of a child then take it up with the social worker.

Single parents

BEING A SINGLE PARENT is about the toughest job around. Who takes it on?

- **By choice.** A girl of sixteen from a dysfunctional home and wanting desperately to love and be loved said, 'I'll get me a baby', and deliberately got pregnant.

- **By death.** A husband died and left his wife with five children and a few months after twins were added to the family. The oldest boy was fifteen.

- **By divorce or separation.** Sometimes the parting is amicable but not often. It is rare that the children are not affected. A man whose parents parted when he was a kid told how 'the pain never goes away'.

- **By not marrying.** When the girl became pregnant the man 'didn't want to know' or she didn't want the child's father as a husband. Or the cohabiting relationship fell apart and she was left on her own with a child.

  There is no doubt that it is best for children to grow up with a mother and father (see section on Divorce), but if that doesn't happen, a child is not necessarily doomed to failure. Most single parents are unwavering in their dogged determination to do their best, and some would put a two-parent family to shame. Many highly successful people had troubled childhoods, and it may have been the need to compensate for early difficulties which drove them to success.

PRESSURES ON SINGLE PARENTS

○ **Time and tiredness.** A single mum cried, 'I used to laugh when people said "for mother read taxi", but I understand it now. I'm *so tired* with endless ferryings to and from school, friends' houses and the youth club, quite apart from my job, shopping and running the home. I love my kids but I never seem to get time for myself.'

○ **Money and worry.** Another mum said, 'How do you run a home on half the money you once had? Benefits? Yes, they help, but there's no week I don't wonder how I'll manage. I worry about everything. Is this rash meningitis? Why is my son not talking to me? Can I trust my daughter? Am I too strict or too soft? Decisions, decisions, decisions; suppose I get them wrong? It's all too much, and the worry is getting me down.'

○ **Loneliness.** A single dad said, 'My daughter was angry with me because I cried so little when her mother left. What she didn't know was how much I cried when she was asleep.' A widow with four young children explained, 'It was not just being alone, it was being lonely and desperately missing companionship.'

COPING AS A SINGLE PARENT

○ **Don't look back.** Don't dwell on what you can't change, may be easy to say and hard to do. But all too often the 'if only' of the past leads to the 'pity me' of the present, which in turn leads into a grey mist of depression. Look up, look out, look forward, but don't look back.

Look up, look out, look forward, but don't look back

- **Ask for help** Don't be ashamed to ask for help with seeking money from a reluctant father, advice for unravelling the mysteries of tax, wisdom for dealing with the latest family crisis, or childminding so you can breathe occasionally. But be careful not to create an unhealthy dependence on your child, so your child is an adult before he knows it.

- **Make time for yourself.** You love your kids to bits and you'll give them all the time you can. But you must keep some for yourself. Don't let yourself go and don't allow yourself to become isolated. You'll be a better parent if you look after yourself properly.

Step families

A husband left his wife and two small children and moved right out of their lives. She married again and her second husband became totally 'Dad'. They knew no other. The difficulty can come if they are older, particularly in their teens. The new husband or wife can be viewed as an intruder and their sharing a bedroom seem like betrayal. Rarely do they become fully Mum or Dad, especially if children are still in contact with their other parent. Continuity with grandparents, the extended family, school and friends is a help in the big adjustment.

The greatest problem comes with the merging of two lots of children. They come with different expectations and sets of rules. It takes a lot of wisdom and patience to blend two families.

BE UNITED. If there was an acrimonious divorce it isn't going to help the children if they hear you and your new partner quarrelling. They may even try to prise you apart. If you think differently on an issue, especially if it's about them, talk to each other before talking to them. Don't criticise their father or mother to them. Even if they agree with you, they'll resent you. Above all let them see your love for each other and let that spill over to them. Respect their need for attention from their resident parent as well as their feelings for their absent mother or father.

BE UNDERSTANDING. One child may tell a step-brother or sister, 'He's *my* Dad' or 'She's *my* Mum.' That's inevitable, as from their point of view they are having to share their mother or father. In your efforts to be accepted by your stepchildren, whatever you do, don't neglect your own 'steps'!

There are no 'steps' in this house except outside the door!

MEMO

NO STEPS IN THIS HOUSE. Take a real interest in your stepchildren and find out what makes them tick. Be aware of their weaknesses and play to their strengths. Be fair. 'I'll treat you exactly the way I treat my own child. If I don't always get it right I'm open to your telling me. There will be no "steps" in this house except the ones outside the door or going upstairs!' Make sure they are included in family decisions.

DON'T RUSH IT. However much you want to be liked and accepted it's going to take time. You can't force your way into their confidence. It's got to grow, and growth is gradual. Sometimes a wonderful bond is formed. One teenager even said to his stepmother, 'The best thing my mother ever did was leaving us. We got you!'

Parents in pain

'HOW ARE THINGS?' 'Fine', your lips say, but your heart says, 'if only they knew!' You wonder if they can see behind the mask which hides your pain, pain of dashed hopes, fear of what the future holds for your family, and perhaps a deep well of parental guilt. It seems a far cry from what you had dreamed when you first cradled them in your arms. What happens?

○ **Financial hardship.** Does unemployment, incapacitating illness or accident mean you cannot provide what you would like, or because of death, desertion or divorce there is one income instead of two?

○ **Handicap.** There is no realistic hope of his ever being better. You worry about how he will cope when you are no longer there. You do not love less because of the handicap; if anything you love more.

○ **Death.** The unimaginable happened and with one swift stroke (or did her life unravel slowly?) you lost her. Even now, years later, memories and tears still catch you unawares.

○ **Estrangement.** How is it possible that the small hand put so trustingly into your large one could one day be clenched in angry defiance? The feet that walked beside yours never come home. There is no familiar handwriting through the door or sound from the telephone. As months crawl into years you have to acknowledge that you have grown apart. But remember relationships are two-sided; do what *you* can.

○ **Major happenings.** A teenage daughter becomes pregnant, a son is on drugs, a girl's life is blighted by an eating disorder or alcohol rules the happy child of earlier years. You hurt with their hurt and you hurt with your own.

WHAT'S TO BE DONE?

DON'T BROOD OVER THE PAST. You can't change it and there may be no answer to your 'why?' But though the past is dead and gone, it can be very much alive in what you *allow* it to do to you now. Over *that* you have power.

○ **You failed as a parent?** Maybe you did, though perhaps their view of you as a mother or father is more positive than yours! Or maybe there's stuff bottled up inside them that is crippling them and they need to release it. They need the opening that *you* make to tell you how *they* hurt. It may be something they misread and for years they have been holding hurt unnecessarily. Or maybe you really did blow it, but unless you talk (or write) you'll not know it. If they say, 'Mum, Dad, when we were growing up …' and out it comes, then you can use that hardest (and best?) word in the language, 'sorry!' The bonding of childhood could begin again.

Forgive or fester

MEMO

○ **The failure was theirs?** It may have been a one-off but of such magnitude that you die inside each time you think about it. Or perhaps you have to admit to yourself you don't actually like the one you love so much. What do you do? 'Tell them off'? That will make it worse. You may choose to say something about how you feel, while acknowledging your own contribution, or you may choose to be silent. But one thing you will do; you'll choose to forgive. It's forgive or fester. Go over and over it in your mind, see it all again, hear it all, feel it all, and you'll destroy yourself and any hope of rebuilding your relationship with son or daughter.

MEMO

Pain shared is pain divided

SHARE YOUR PAIN. Somewhere there is someone with whom you can share your pain. Notice, some*one*, or a small circle of trusted ones. Not everyone. A woman, terribly hurt, told all her friends about it who cried, 'Poor you!' 'That's exactly what I wanted to hear,' she later confessed, 'but their sympathy fed my hate.' Tell everyone and you'll deepen and prolong your pain.

Psychiatrist Dr John White rightly said, 'Pain shared is pain divided', but as it is difficult to share family pain *within* the family because it is *about* family, you may choose someone *outside* the family. Out there there's someone worthy of trust who will not betray your confidence. Someone who takes seriously the biblical words 'Carry each other's burdens' (Galatians 6:2) and will help to carry yours. Find that someone.

BUILD ON THE ROCK. Not everyone does this but anyone can. Jesus told the story of two men, each building a house (Luke 6:46–49). One 'dug down deep and laid the foundation on rock'. The other, no doubt in a hurry, 'built a house on the ground without a foundation'. When the storm struck and the flood came it 'could not shake' the house built on rock. Of the second, built carelessly with no foundation, the record states simply, 'it collapsed'. The story is a parable of faith and practice. Jesus said that the one who built on rock is the one 'who comes to me and hears my words and puts them into practice'. What could be more personal? Storms strike every life; some stand firm and some collapse. Check your foundations.

Gaining maturity

G

12m

as the 'children' mature; roots and wings;
looking after yourself; role of the grandparents; making good memories

Gaining maturity

You've been working towards their independence for years. Remember when your crawler first stood up with that look of delighted surprise on his face, wobbled, and promptly sat down? Since then there have been a thousand ups and downs until now, in every sense, he stands on his own feet.

The 'child' matures

ROOTS AND WINGS. You gave your children *roots* in the love you poured out on them and which was absorbed into every pore of their being. They knew they belonged. Now is the time for *wings*. It is not enough for them to move geographically out of your home or to the other side of the world, they must move emotionally. As they gradually matured, you gave, and they gained, more and more independence, and as they gained independence that itself brought maturity. It can be summed up like this: as they grow you let them go, and as they go, they grow!

MEMO

As they grow you let them go, as they go, they grow!

One of the signs of maturity is when they see you weren't so bad after all!

Mark Twain laughed, 'When I was a boy of fourteen, my father was so ignorant I could hardly stand to have the old man around. But when I got to be twenty-one, I was astonished at how much the old man had learned in seven years.' (Attributed)

DEVELOPMENT OF CHARACTER. Over her growing years she has made choices, and choices have made character. Her views and values may be the same as yours or may be different. That is not something you can control. But a clearly identifiable person has emerged. Her genes were from her parents but her character is her own.

She may be eighteen and legally an adult but that character is not yet fully developed. She, and you, must make allowance for that.

FINANCIAL SUPPORT. Because of further education and in some cases years of training for professional qualifications, it may be necessary for parents to continue to support their children financially. Or if they are earning and living at home they'll probably contribute to the running of the home. They'll appreciate it more if they do.

LIVING AT HOME. Education, saving for buying their own property, the benefits of 'mum's cooking', or simply because they like living at home, means perhaps they stay on. If they do, they should on the one hand share household chores, and on the other respect their parents' values. They may be entitled to vote but they are not entitled to ride roughshod over their parents' feelings. It is still *your* home.

Maturity of the parent

LOOK AFTER YOURSELF. If you love your child, look after yourself. Aim at being a super mum and you'll probably end up being a super martyr, which is painful for you and everyone else. Don't stuff or starve yourself; eat sensibly. It's tough if you're on your own, but try to get enough sleep, rest, exercise and fun. *Make* time to read the paper, curl up with a book or whatever is 'you time'. It may sound strange, but you can be too unselfish, which is not good for your child – or you. Remember that parents are people too.

Parent and toddler groups give the opportunity for adult company and conversation while your child is in a safe place. Many churches have a crèche so parents are free to join in worship with others in the congregation. Some have cell group meetings, usually in homes, for prayer, study, fellowship and encouragement. Whatever you do in your commitment to being a good parent, don't become isolated. Have interests and friends outside the family.

> **MEMO**
>
> **There is no greater gift you can give your children than to love each other**

LOOK AFTER YOUR MARRIAGE. Children can drive partners apart or draw them together.

In the authors' book *The Highway Code for Marriage* (CWR), you will find a sevenfold secret of good marriage – communication, affection, respect, encouragement, forgiveness, unselfishness and loyalty. These words make the acrostic CAREFUL. You take care crossing the road or you may not reach the other side. You take care of your health or you may not survive. Take care of your marriage. The better you are as a partner the better you'll be as a parent, and there is no greater gift you can give your children than to love each other.

With all the time you give to the family make time for each other. Go out without the children. A 'minimoon' of a day or two doesn't have to be expensive. Grandparents or friends will look after the children. Some conscientious parents ask if it's fair to leave the children, and the answer is a resounding 'yes' for three reasons. They'll appreciate you more when you come back, it makes them more secure as they learn that you *will* come back, and what's good for your marriage is good for them.

SHARE YOUR PARENTING. They need a mother *and* father. Back each other up. Let one do something with the children while the other sleeps. Take turns if possible so that it isn't always the same parent who puts them to bed, checks homework and chores, disciplines or does fun stuff with them. Put a family holiday together high on your list of priorities. The memories will last a lifetime.

Grandparents – second time round

When your children have children you can, as they say, 'enjoy them and give 'em back'. That's the theory but sometimes it doesn't work out like that. Grandmothers fill in as carers for working mums and many lone parents live with the children's grandparents. Research shows that grandparents are often cited as more important to the children than absent parents. Sometimes they are able to give what a parent couldn't. One woman in her fifties looking back to her childhood when there was little affection shown by her parents to her, said wistfully of her grandfather, 'His are the arms I remember.'

Grandparents have found the following principles useful:

○ **Available but not exploited.** A grandmother put it like this, 'I used to be *always* available to help with the kids, and did a lot of childminding which I was happy to do and which I loved. Still do! But increasingly I felt I was being taken for granted. Today I'm still glad to help out but it's what I call a measured availability. *Always* is now *sometimes*.'

○ **Supportive but not intrusive.** They may make mistakes in their parenting (you did too) but be careful when (or if!) you say anything. It can be taken as intrusion. If you do speak then casual *suggestion* is better than *correction* – 'Do you think Jamie might …?' The children are theirs not yours, and your job is to back them up for all you're worth. If you see something good, say it to the children. 'That was really kind of your Mum and Dad. You're lucky to have parents like that.' And say to their parents, 'I admire the way you handled that …' or 'We think you're doing a great job.' They'll appreciate your support. And remember always that grandparents need to learn the delicate balance between hands on and hands off.

○ **Loving but not demanding.** In an uncertain and confusing world your love for the family is something utterly solid and dependable. That's good, keep it that way. But as you get older don't get to the stage that you are demanding time from your young people or grandchildren as payment for past services! Never let 'You owe it to me' pass your lips or even lodge in your mind.

○ **Sharing and not competing.** Accept that the grandparents on the other side of the family also love the kids. Don't compete with them in time or with presents, and aim to speak of them to your grandchildren with respect.

Look to the future

○ **Family.** You've met grumbling grannies and crotchety granddads and you don't want to be like them. Choose to be positive, choose to be grateful, choose to be flexible, choose to care, encourage and love. You can add warmth and width to their lives. Resolve to be a blessing not a burden to your family.

○ **Finance.** A husband and wife in their wills had made arrangements in event of their death for the care of their 'infant children', but years later when they checked their wills the 'infants' were young adults. Is your will up-to-date? If the unexpected happens can documents relating to property and monies be easily found? Months can be lost and distress greatly increased because nobody knows where to find anything.

o **Friends.** It's good to have friends so that you are not entirely dependent on family. People age rapidly if they are isolated. There is an old saying, 'I went out to find a friend and did not find one there; I went out to be a friend and found friends everywhere.' Choose to make friends, for good friendships keep you resilient and strong; and keep those friendships in good repair. The psychiatrist, John White, who said, 'Pain shared is pain divided' added, 'Pleasure shared is pleasure multiplied.'

Pleasure shared is pleasure multiplied

MEMO

o **Fitness.** Your brain is not like a computer that you can leave unused and after a year find it is working just as well. It needs to be stretched with an input of information and an output of conversation. 'Use it or lose it' applies to body and brain alike. Both need regular exercise and a balanced diet for good mental and physical health.

Enjoying the family

RELIVING THE YEARS. One day you may forget where you put your teeth or that they have heard that story 125 times already. But you'll relive your children's laughter as if it were yesterday, you'll feel their hand in yours, their first day at school, rolling on the floor with them, the triumph in their eyes when they swam their first length. You'll recall things they said, problems they shared with you, holidays together, the day they left home for a new life of their own. What will *they* remember? Not so much the things you did *for* them as the things you did *with* them.

MAKE GOOD MEMORIES. Make good memories for yourself and your children. When they are small they want your eyes to watch them on their next adventure, your ears to listen to their fears and joys, your lips to reassure, your hands to show them how, your feet to go where they go and your heart to love them. In a word they want *you*. When they are bigger, stronger, wiser and independent, they don't need you in the same way, but they still want to be sure that you love them and that you are proud of them. Let them know it.

A mature man writing to his parents on their wedding anniversary, said 'Thank you for a lifetime of encouragement, and as life moves on I appreciate all the more the richness of my childhood and the family life we enjoyed together. The children are fortunate to have such grandparents and we all wish you many more good years together.' While life lasts those words will live. It's a privilege to be a parent. Enjoy it.

National Distributors

UK: (and countries not listed below)
CWR, Waverley Abbey House, Waverley Lane, Farnham, Surrey GU9 8EP.
Tel: (01252) 784700 Outside UK (+44) 1252 784700

AUSTRALIA: CMC Australasia, PO Box 519, Belmont, Victoria 3216.
Tel: (03) 5241 3288 Fax: (03) 5241 3290

CANADA: Cook Communications Ministries, PO Box 98, 55 Woodslee
Avenue, Paris, Ontario N3L 3E5. Tel: 1800 263 2664

GHANA: Challenge Enterprises of Ghana, PO Box 5723, Accra.
Tel: (021) 222437/223249 Fax: (021) 226227

HONG KONG: Cross Communications Ltd, 1/F, 562A Nathan Road, Kowloon.
Tel: 2780 1188 Fax: 2770 6229

INDIA: Crystal Communications, 10-3-18/4/1, East Marredpalli, Secunderabad
– 500026, Andhra Pradesh. Tel/Fax: (040) 27737145

KENYA: Keswick Books and Gifts Ltd, PO Box 10242, Nairobi.
Tel: (02) 331692/226047 Fax: (02) 728557

MALAYSIA: Salvation Book Centre (M) Sdn Bhd, 23 Jalan SS 2/64,
47300 Petaling Jaya, Selangor. Tel: (03) 78766411/78766797 Fax: (03)
78757066/78756360

NEW ZEALAND: CMC Australasia, PO Box 36015, Lower Hutt.
Tel: 0800 449 408 Fax: 0800 449 049

NIGERIA: FBFM, Helen Baugh House, 96 St Finbarr's College Road, Akoka,
Lagos.
Tel: (01) 7747429/4700218/825775/827264

PHILIPPINES: OMF Literature Inc, 776 Boni Avenue, Mandaluyong City.
Tel: (02) 531 2183 Fax: (02) 531 1960

SOUTH AFRICA: Struik Christian Books, 80 MacKenzie Street, PO Box 1144,
Cape Town 8000. Tel: (021) 462 4360 Fax: (021) 461 3612

SRI LANKA: Christombu Publications (Pvt) Ltd., Bartleet House, 65
Braybrooke Place, Colombo 2. Tel: (9411) 2421073/2447665

TANZANIA: CLC Christian Book Centre, PO Box 1384, Mkwepu Street, Dar
es Salaam. Tel/Fax: (022) 2119439

USA: Cook Communications Ministries, PO Box 98, 55 Woodslee Avenue,
Paris, Ontario N3L 3E5, Canada. Tel: 1800 263 2664

ZIMBABWE: Word of Life Books (Pvt) Ltd, Christian Media Centre, 8
Aberdeen Road, Avondale, PO Box A480 Avondale, Harare. Tel: (04) 333355 or
091301188

For email addresses, visit the CWR website: www.cwr.org.uk

CWR is a registered charity – Number 294387

**CWR is a limited company registered in England – Registration
Number 1990308**

Day and Residential Courses
Counselling Training
Leadership Development
Biblical Study Courses
Regional Seminars
Ministry to Women
Daily Devotionals
Books and Videos
Conference Centre

Trusted all Over the World

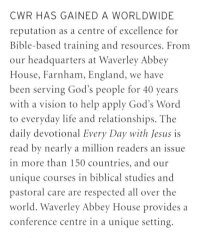

CWR HAS GAINED A WORLDWIDE reputation as a centre of excellence for Bible-based training and resources. From our headquarters at Waverley Abbey House, Farnham, England, we have been serving God's people for 40 years with a vision to help apply God's Word to everyday life and relationships. The daily devotional *Every Day with Jesus* is read by nearly a million readers an issue in more than 150 countries, and our unique courses in biblical studies and pastoral care are respected all over the world. Waverley Abbey House provides a conference centre in a unique setting.

For free brochures on our seminars and courses, conference facilities, or a catalogue of CWR resources, please contact us at the following address:

CWR, Waverley Abbey House, Waverley Lane, Farnham, Surrey GU9 8EP, UK

Telephone: +44 (0)1252 784700
Email: mail@cwr.org.uk
Website: www.cwr.org.uk

The Highway Code for Marriage

Michael and Hilary Perrott

Are you about to get married? Are you thinking of giving up on your marriage? Or do you just want to make your marriage better? Whatever your situation, this book can help. Tackling the highs and lows of relationships, *The Highway Code for Marriage* is an honest, often humorous and definitely hope-filled book.

£6.99 (plus p&p)

ISBN: 978-1-85345-331-1

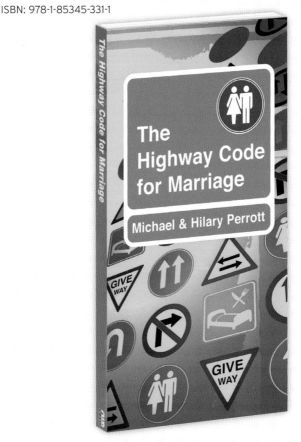

Price correct at time of printing

Just Do It

Michael and Hilary Perrott

A book for those who constantly put off till tomorrow what they should do today! The writers show that procrastination can even be dangerous, as for example when we don't get round to buying that smoke alarm. But we can choose to change, and that is what this book is all about – decide to get on and just do it!

£6.99 (plus p&p)
ISBN: 978-1-85345-392-2

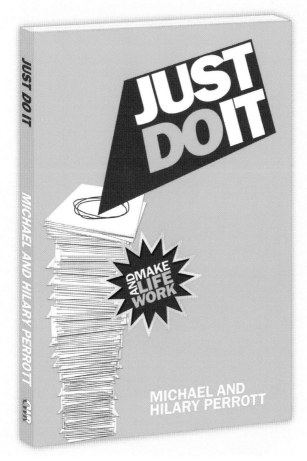

Waverley Abbey Insight Series:
Insight into Self-esteem

Chris Ledger and Wendy Bray

How do we judge ourselves? As Christians, we find our true value and worth in God. This book draws on a wealth of practical experience to show how growing our relationship with God through Jesus can banish our feelings of low self-esteem.

ISBN: 978-1-85345-409-7

Other books in this series:

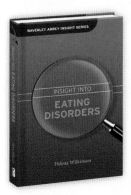

Insight into Eating Disorders
Helena Wilkinson
ISBN: 978-1-85345-410-3

Insight into Stress
Beverley Shepherd
ISBN: 978-1-85345-384-7

Insight into Bereavement
Wendy Bray and Diana Priest
ISBN: 978-1-85345-385-4

£7.50 each (plus p&p)

Prices correct at time of printing